Better Homes and Gardens
STEP-BY-STEP
Plumbing

Better Homes and Gardens® Books
Des Moines, Iowa

Better Homes and Gardens® Books
An imprint of Meredith® Books

Step-by-Step Plumbing
Editor: Benjamin W. Allen
Associate Art Director: Tom Wegner
Copy Chief: Angela K. Renkoski
Electronic Production Coordinator: Paula Forest
Editorial Assistant: Susan McBroom
Design Assistant: Jennifer Norris
Production Manager: Douglas Johnston
Prepress Coordinator: Marjorie J. Schenkelberg

Meredith® Books
Editor in Chief: James D. Blume
Managing Editor: Christopher Cavanaugh
Editor, Shelter Books: Denise L. Caringer
Director, New Product Development: Ray Wolf
Vice President, General Manager: Jamie L. Martin

Better Homes and Gardens® **Magazine**
Editor in Chief: Jean LemMon
Executive Building Editor: Joan McCloskey

Meredith Publishing Group
President, Publishing Group: Christopher Little
Vice President and Publishing Director: John P. Loughlin

Meredith Corporation
Chairman of the Board and Chief Executive Officer: Jack D. Rehm
President and Chief Operating Officer: William T. Kerr
Chairman of the Executive Committee: E. T. Meredith III

Produced by Greenleaf Publishing, Inc.
Publishing Director: Dave Toht
Associate Editor: Steve Cory
Assistant Editor: Rebecca JonMichaels
Design: Melanie Lawson Design
Illustrations: Brian Gilmer and Stuart Zastro, Art Factory
Technical Consultants: Steve Mendel, Mendel Plumbing, St. Charles, Illinois

Cover photograph: Tony Kubat Photography
On the cover: A Moen® "Monticello" lever-handle chrome faucet

All of us at Better Homes and Gardens® Books are dedicated to providing you with information and ideas you need to enhance your home. We welcome your comments and suggestions about this book on plumbing. Write to us at: Better Homes and Gardens® Books, Do-It-Yourself Editorial Department, RW–206, 1716 Locust St., Des Moines, IA 50309–3023.

Note to the Reader: Due to differing conditions, tools, and individual skills, Meredith Corporation assumes no responsibility for any damages, injuries suffered, or losses incurred as a result of following the information published in this book. Before beginning any project, review the instructions carefully, and if any doubts or questions remain, consult local experts or authorities. Because local codes and regulations vary greatly, you always should check with local authorities to ensure that your project complies with all applicable local codes and regulations. Always read and observe all of the safety precautions provided by any tool or equipment manufacturer, and follow all accepted safety procedures.

TABLE OF CONTENTS

Basics

Introduction 4
Getting to Know Your System. 6
Supply System. 7
Drain System. 8
Vent System 9

Tools and Materials

Essential Tools. 10
Specialized Tools 11
Choosing Pipe. 12
Choosing the Right Fitting 14
Measuring Pipes and Fittings 16

Skills

Working with Rigid Copper Pipe 18
Working with Flexible Copper Tubing 21
Using Compression Fittings 22
Using Flare Fittings 23
Removing Old Threaded Pipe. 24
Installing Threaded Pipe 25
Working with Rigid Plastic Pipe 26
Working with Flexible Plastic Tubing 28
Quieting Noisy Pipes 29

Minor Improvements and Repairs

Installing Stop Valves. 30
Troubleshooting Main Line Valves. 31
Preventing Freeze-Ups 32
Winterizing a House 33
Fixing Leaks and Frozen Pipes 34
Identifying Stem Faucets 36
Pulling Out Handles and Stems 37
Replacing Seat Washers 37
Repairing Diaphragm and Cartridge Stems . . . 38
Repairing Leaks from Handles 38
Replacing and Grinding Seats. 39
Repairing Cartridge Faucets 40
Repairing Rotating Ball Faucets 42
Repairing Ceramic Disk Faucets 44
Repairing Gasketed Cartridge Faucets. 46
Sealing Leaky Base Plates 47
Fixing Sprayers, Diverters, and Aerators 48
Stopping Leaks in Flexible Supply Lines 49
Replacing Faucets 50
Repairing Toilets 52
Fixing Tank Run-On 53
Fixing Leaky Tanks and Bowls 55

Replacing Toilets 56
Maintaining and Fixing Water Heaters 58
Repairing Electric Water Heaters. 60
Repairing Gas Water Heaters 61
Replacing Gas Water Heaters 62
Replacing Electric Water Heaters 65
Repairing Tub and Shower Controls 66
Replacing Bathtubs 68
Opening Clogged Drains 70
Using Simple Unclogging Methods 71
Dismantling Fixture Traps 72
Replacing Sink Strainers. 73
Augering Techniques 74
Unclogging Showers 74
Unclogging Tubs 75
Cleaning Drum Traps. 75
Unclogging Toilets 76
Clearing Main Drains and Sewer Lines 77
Adjusting Drain Assemblies 78
Cleaning Showerheads 79

Major Improvements

Planning for New Fixtures 80
Venting Possibilities. 81
Roughing in Tubs, Showers, and Toilets 82
Tapping into Existing Lines 84
Adding Plastic Drain Lines 86
Tapping into Cast-Iron Drain Lines. 87
Adding New Vents 88
Running the Supply Lines 89
Installing Rimmed Sinks 90
Installing Wall-Hung Sinks. 92
Installing Pedestal Sinks. 93
Adding Vanities 93
Installing Showers 94
Installing Prefab Units 95
Preparing for Tile. 95
Installing Hand Showers 96
Installing Water Filtration Systems 97
Installing Whole-House Filters 97
Installing Under-Sink Filtration Units 98
Choosing Water Softeners 99
Plumbing Icemakers 100
Installing Garbage Disposals 101
Maintaining Garbage Disposals. 103
Replacing and Installing Dishwashers 104
Installing Hot Water Dispensers 106

Glossary 108
Index 110
Metric Conversions 112

INTRODUCTION

Whether it's a dripping faucet or a complete bathroom remodeling, if you own a home, you'll eventually face some sort of plumbing job. Most people assume plumbing is dirty and difficult, requiring skills gained only by years of experience. Fear of the unknown drives them to pay hundreds and even thousands of dollars to plumbers to do jobs they might easily handle themselves. Even when homeowners hire out jobs legitimately beyond their skill level, they're often in the dark about whether the job has been done right—and for a fair price.

Step-by-Step Plumbing explains how your plumbing system works and what it takes to tackle most household repairs and improvements. It will show you, in step-by-step fashion, how to fix minor and major problems and how to install new plumbing fixtures in a professional manner.

Perhaps best of all, Step-by-Step Plumbing will help you evaluate what you can take on yourself. You'll find that plumbing can be a budget-sparing and satisfying way to improve your home. If you choose to call in the pros, you'll be equipped to manage the job wisely.

Working to Code

Even though you may be an amateur working on your own house, you have the same responsibilities as a licensed plumber. The plumbing you repair or install must provide a supply of pure and wholesome water, and must facilitate the safe passage of liquids, solid wastes, and gases out of your house. That means using only those techniques and materials that are acceptable to the building codes of your area.

The procedures in this book represent the editors' understanding of the Uniform Plumbing Code (UPC). Local codes are based on this uniform code but can vary greatly from each other. If there are no local codes covering the work you will be doing, consult the national codes. Ask your reference librarian to see the latest edition of the UPC. If local codes cover your project, they supersede any national requirements. (Canadian residents may obtain a copy of the Canadian Plumbing Code by contacting Publications Sales M-20, National Research Council of Canada, Ottawa, K1A 0R6 Ontario.)

Working with Your Local Building Department

Always check with your local building department if you are considering adding or changing your plumbing in any substantial way or if you believe the existing plumbing might be substandard. Plumbing codes may seem bothersome, but they are designed to make your home's plumbing system safe and worry-free. Ignoring codes can lead to costly mistakes, health hazards, and even difficulties in someday selling your house.

If you will be adding new service—not just replacing one fixture with another one—check with your building department before proceeding. Neglecting to do so could cause you the expense and trouble of tearing out and redoing your work.

There's no telling what kind of inspector you will get: He or she could be helpful, friendly, and flexible, or a real stickler. But no matter what sort of personality you'll be dealing with, your work will go better if you follow these guidelines:

■ To avoid unnecessary questions, find out as much information as possible about your project before you talk to an inspector. Your building department may have literature concerning your type of installation. If not, consult national codes.

■ Go to your inspector with a plan to be approved or amended; don't expect the building department to plan the job for you.

■ Present your plan with neatly drawn diagrams and a complete list of the materials you will be using.

■ Be sure you clearly understand when you need to have inspections. Do not cover up any work that needs to be inspected.

■ Be as courteous as possible. Inspectors are often wary of homeowners, because so many do shoddy work. Show the inspector you are serious about doing things the right way, and comply with any requirements without arguing.

How to Use This Book

*B*egin by reading the first section, "Basics." This will give you the general knowledge you need to help you understand specific parts of your plumbing system. If you plan to do some plumbing work yourself, read only the pages of the next sections, "Tools and Materials" and "Skills," that apply to you. For instance, there's no need to read about cast-iron pipe if your house doesn't have any.

The rest of the book deals with specific repairs and installations, some of which you'll be facing in your home. When a problem arises, consult the section "Minor Improvements and Repairs" for help with how to fix a faucet, repair a water heater, clear out a clog in your bathtub, or fix most anything else that can go wrong with household plumbing.

If you want to make a serious upgrade of your home's plumbing, the "Major Improvements" section will help you plan, budget, and complete jobs you may have thought only the pros should handle. If you have the time and energy, there is virtually no installation you cannot make—or job you cannot understand should you choose to hire a professional.

Feature Boxes

*I*n addition to basic instructions, you'll find plenty of tips throughout the book. For every project, a You'll Need box tells you how long the project will take, what skills are necessary, and what tools you must have. The other tip boxes shown on this page provide practical help to ensure that the plumbing work you do will be as pleasurable as possible, and that it will result in safe and long-lasting improvements to your home.

MEASUREMENTS

Keep an eye out for this box when standard measurements, critical tolerances, or special measuring techniques are called for.

Money $ Saver

Throwing money at a job does not necessarily make it a better one. Money Saver helps cut your costs with tips on how to accurately estimate your material needs, make wise tool purchases, and organize the job to minimize wasted labor.

EXPERTS' INSIGHT

Tricks of the trade can make all the difference in helping you do a job quickly and well. Experts' Insight gives insiders' tips on methods and materials that make the job easier.

CAUTION!
When a how-to step requires special care, Caution! warns you what to watch out for. It will help keep you from doing damage to yourself or the job at hand.

TOOLS TO USE

If you'll need special tools not commonly found in a home-owner's toolbox, we'll tell you about them in Tools to Use.

GETTING TO KNOW YOUR SYSTEM

With so many pipes and fittings running unseen inside walls and floors, a plumbing system can seem complicated and mysterious. But plumbing is actually a straightforward matter of distributing incoming water to where it's wanted and facilitating the outflow of waste. Here's an overview of how household plumbing works.

Supply, drain, and vent systems

The supply system brings water into your house, divides it into hot and cold water lines, and distributes it to various fixtures (sinks, toilets, showers, tubs) and appliances (washing machines, dishwashers, water heaters, heating system boilers).

The drain system carries water away from the fixtures and appliances, and out of the house. The vent system supplies air to the drain pipes so waste flows out freely. Because drains and vents use the same types of pipes and are tied together, they often are referred to as the drain-waste-vent system, or DWV.

Locating the water meter and main shutoffs

The first step toward gaining mastery over your house's plumbing system is to locate the water meter and, more important, the main shutoff.

Look for the place where water first enters your house. Usually, you'll find a pipe an inch or so thick, called a water main, coming up through the floor in your basement or first floor. If you have metered water, the pipe will enter and exit a round gauge, the water meter. This has either a digital readout that looks like a car's odometer or a series of five or six dials. The meter tells how much water passes into the house. If you have a well, or if your bill does not change no matter how much water you use, you don't have a meter.

Near the place where the water main enters your house, look for one or two valves that you can turn on and off by hand. This is the main shutoff for the house.

You may have an additional shutoff outside the house, buried in a cavity sometimes called a "buffalo box." To find it, look for a round metal cover in the ground near the street or the edge of your property. It may be overgrown with grass. Pry it up and look inside with a flashlight. There may be a valve that you can turn by hand, or you may need a special long-handled "key." Older homes in warm weather locations sometimes have an exposed valve just outside the house.

If you have an older home, don't depend entirely on the inside shutoff; it can break, leak, or stop shutting off completely. If you'll have to shut down the system often during a project, learn where your outside shutoff is and use it to shut off the water.

CAUTION!
ALWAYS BE PREPARED TO SHUT OFF THE WATER

In case of a burst pipe or other emergency, be ready to shut off the main water supply quickly. Let members of your family know where the main shutoff is. Clear away boxes and furniture so it is easy to get at. If it takes a special tool to shut off your water, keep it handy.

WHERE YOUR RESPONSIBILITY ENDS

The water meter is the continental divide when it comes to assigning responsibility for plumbing repairs. The water meter and pipes leading away from the house are the responsibility of the water company. They should fix them for free. Anything on the house side of the meter is your responsibility. However, if you will be adding new fixtures (not just replacing old ones), your municipality may require a larger water main coming into the house. If so, you'll have to pay for it. Check when you get your permit.

THE NEW AND THE OLD

In the old days, plumbers installed cast-iron drain lines. They had to pack each joint with tarred oakum, then pour in molten lead—a practice dating from the time of the Romans. For supply lines and smaller drain lines, they used galvanized pipe, which is strong but can rust and corrode over time.

Plastic drain lines and copper supply lines are superior to the old materials. They last much longer and are easier to work with. However, it took many years for different localities to make the switch to modern materials. In some places, for instance, cast-iron was required by code well into the 1980s. And to this day, some municipalities require that supply lines be made with galvanized pipe.

If you have old pipe, there's no need to rip it out. Many products are available that make it easy to connect the new to the old. These products often use rubber gaskets that will remain leakproof for many decades.

SUPPLY SYSTEM

Water enters your house through a pipe that connects either to a municipal water line or a private well. If your bill changes according to how much water you use, your water flows through a water meter. Near the meter you will find one or two main shutoffs.

From there, water travels to the water heater. Water from a private well goes to a pressure tank before going to the heater.

From the water heater, a pair of water lines—one hot and one cold—branch out through the house to serve the various fixtures (toilets, tubs, sinks, showers) and water-using appliances (dishwashers, washing machines, heating system boilers).

These supply lines are always under pressure; if they are opened or a break occurs, water will shoot out and not stop until it is shut off in some way. That is why modern homes have stop (or shutoff) valves for every fixture and appliance. If your home is not equipped with them, plan to install them. They'll make maintenance and repairs more convenient and will more than pay for themselves should you face a serious break.

Older homes have plumbing systems that use galvanized pipe, which will corrode over time, leading to low pressure and leaks. Newer homes use copper and plastic supply lines, which last much longer.

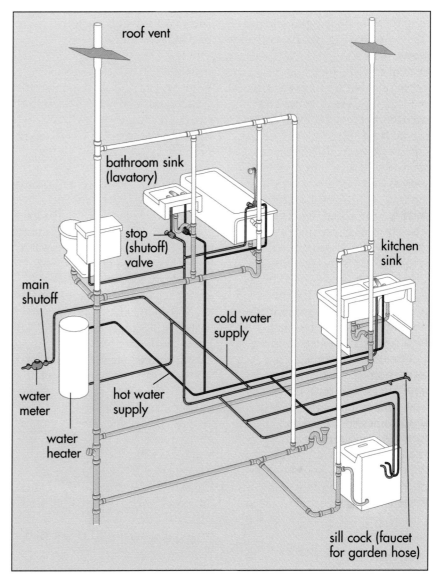

roof vent

bathroom sink (lavatory)

stop (shutoff) valve

kitchen sink

main shutoff

cold water supply

water meter

hot water supply

water heater

sill cock (faucet for garden hose)

SUPPLY SYSTEM PROBLEM SOLVER

For answers to these problems and questions   **see pages**

burst or leaking pipes 34–35
installing stop valves 30–31
new supply lines 89
noisy pipes 29
preventing frozen pipes 32–33
removing and installing pipes and fittings . . .18–28
repairing faucets 36–51
types, sizes of pipes and fittings 12–15
water filters 97–98
water heaters 58–65

DRAIN SYSTEM

Drain pipes use gravity to rid the house of liquid and solid waste. This system also guards against foul-smelling and potentially harmful gases entering the house from the municipal drain system or the septic field.

All fixtures except the toilet empty into a trap (toilets have built-in traps). A trap is a curved section of drain pipe that holds enough standing water to make an airtight seal, which prevents sewer gases from backing up and leaking into the home. Each time a fixture is used, the old water in the trap is forced down the line and replaced with new water.

After leaving the trap, drain water moves in pipes sloped at no less than $\frac{1}{4}$ inch per foot toward a waste stack (also called a soil pipe), a large, vertical pipe that carries water below the floor. There it takes a bend and proceeds out to a municipal sewer line or a private septic system. A clean-out is a place where you can insert an auger to clear the line. Traps serve the same function.

Drain pipes come in $1\frac{1}{4}$-inch pipe for a bathroom sink, $1\frac{1}{2}$-inch for kitchen sinks and bathtubs, and 3- or 4-inch for toilets. The stack is usually a 4-inch pipe. Older homes use cast-iron pipe for the stacks and galvanized pipe for the other drain lines. New homes use plastic, and occasionally copper, for stacks and drains.

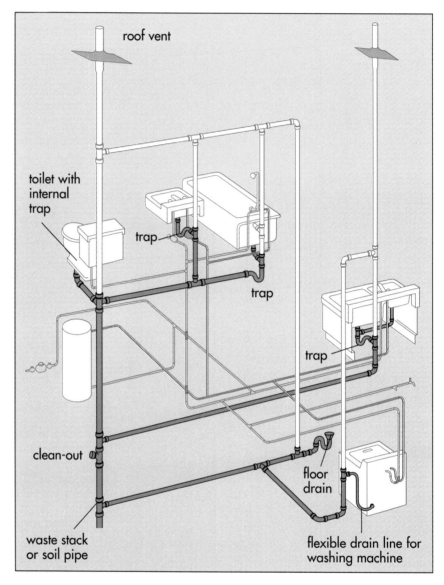

roof vent

toilet with internal trap

trap

trap

trap

clean-out

floor drain

waste stack or soil pipe

flexible drain line for washing machine

DRAIN SYSTEM PROBLEM SOLVER

For answers to these problems and questions   **see pages**

adding a plastic drain line 86
clogged drains 70–77
drain assemblies 78
new garbage disposal 101–103
planning new drain lines 80–83
tapping into drain lines 84–85
toilets 52–57
tying in to a cast-iron drain line 87
types of pipe and fittings 12–15
working with plastic pipe and tubing 26–28

VENT SYSTEM

*T*o flow freely, drain pipes need air. Without air, water will glug down a drain like soda pop from a bottle. A plumbing vent plays the same role as that little second opening in a gasoline can. With the stopper closed, gas pours out slowly. But once the stopper is opened, the air entering the can allows the liquid to flow freely.

Also, the air supplied by a vent prevents siphoning action, which might otherwise pull water up out of traps and toilets and allow sewage gases to escape into the house. Instead, vents carry the gases through your roof. Sewer gas, composed largely of methane, is not only smelly, it is harmful and dangerous. Don't be tempted to install a substandard venting system, even if it means avoiding a lot of work.

A main vent is an extension of the waste stack and reaches upward through the roof. Branch vents tie into the main vent. Each and every plumbing fixture and appliance must be vented properly, either by tying into a main vent or by having a vent of its own that extends through the roof.

When installing a new fixture in a new location (not just replacing an existing fixture), venting is often the most difficult problem to overcome. Local codes require that venting adhere to specific dimension requirements. Research these requirements before you begin planning. Vent pipes are made of the same materials as drain pipes, although sometimes they are of smaller dimensions.

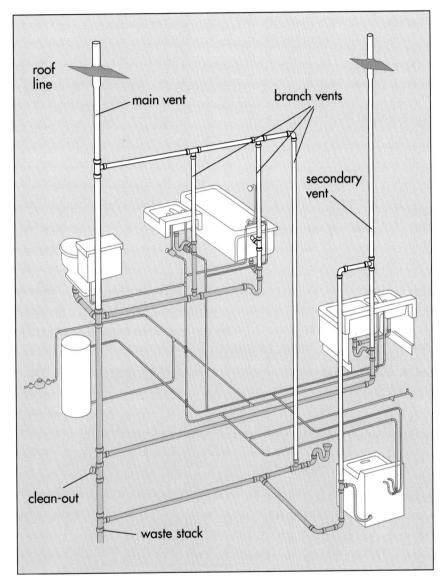

VENT SYSTEM PROBLEM SOLVER

For answers to these problems and questions — **see pages**

adding a new vent 88
fittings for vents .14–15
planning drains and vents 80–81
roof flashing for a vent 88
tapping new vents into old 84–86
tying a new plastic vent into a cast-iron vent . . .87
types of pipe used for venting 12–13
"wet venting" 81
working with plastic pipe 26–27

ESSENTIAL TOOLS

Plumbing does not require a lot of expensive tools, and even those that you may use for only one job are well worth the cost. The money you save by doing your own work will pay for them many times over. Using the tools shown on this page, you can tackle most plumbing projects.

To clear drain lines, get a **plunger.** The type shown here, with the extra flange extending downward, is ideal for toilets and also works well on bathtubs and sinks. Use a hand-cranked **drain auger** to clear away clogs that

won't plunge away. For toilets, use a **closet auger**.

To disassemble and connect pipes and to make a myriad of plumbing repairs, purchase a pair of high-quality **tongue-and-groove pliers**, which adjust to grab almost any size pipe. A standard **adjustable pipe wrench** is essential for working with threaded iron pipe. An **adjustable Crescent wrench** will fit the nuts on faucets and other fixtures.

To cut pipe, use a **hacksaw**. Hacksaw blades dull quickly so have extra blades available.

For running new pipes through walls, you will need a **drill** with plenty of **spade bits**. To cut away drywall or plaster to make room for the plumbing, use a **keyhole saw**. A **flashlight** comes in handy when you need to peer into wall cavities and under sinks.

For delicate chores such as removing faucet O-rings and clips, have a pair of **needle-nose pliers** on hand. And have a ready supply of general-purpose tools, including **screwdrivers**, a **putty knife**, a **utility knife**, and a **tape measure**.

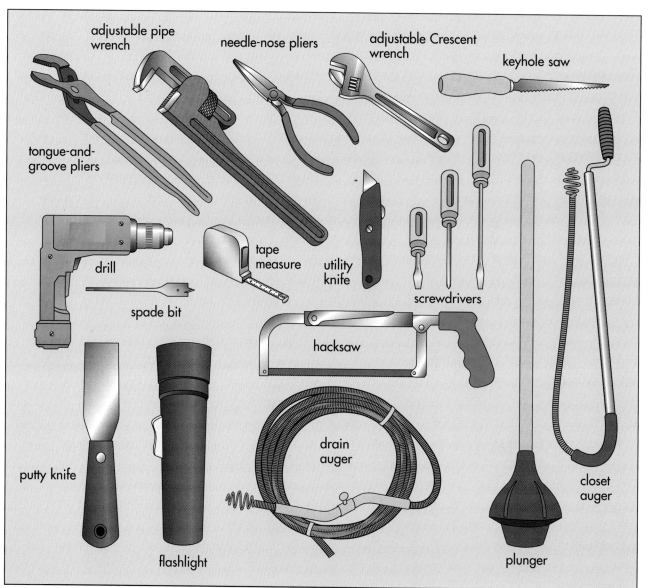

adjustable pipe wrench

needle-nose pliers

adjustable Crescent wrench

keyhole saw

tongue-and-groove pliers

drill

spade bit

tape measure

utility knife

screwdrivers

hacksaw

putty knife

drain auger

closet auger

flashlight

plunger

SPECIALIZED TOOLS

Some tools are designed for specialized plumbing tasks. Choose the ones that will help you work with your materials and fixtures.

If you will be soldering copper pipe, you must have a **propane torch.** If you have a lot to do, pay the extra money for a self-igniting model. Otherwise, get an inexpensive **spark lighter.**

To bend flexible copper tubing without kinking it, use a **tubing bender.** A two-part **flaring tool** is necessary if you want to make flare joints in copper tubing. If

you plan on cutting copper pipe or tubing, buy a **tubing cutter.** It makes easier and cleaner cuts than a **hacksaw** and will not squeeze tubing out of shape. For cutting plastic supply pipes, a **plastic tubing cutter** makes the job easier. To set the proper incline for drain pipes, you'll need a **level.**

When working on faucets and sinks, you will sometimes need a **basin wrench** to get at nuts you cannot reach with pliers. If you have a damaged faucet seat that needs replacing, don't take a chance with a screwdriver—use a

seat wrench. For those big nuts that hold on the basket strainers of kitchen sinks, you may need a **spud wrench.**

When plunging and augering don't clear out a clog, a **blow bag** will often do the trick: hook up a garden hose to it, insert it into the drain pipe, and turn on the water.

For large-scale demolition, notching studs and joists, and quickly cutting galvanized pipe, a **reciprocating saw** makes the job much easier. If you need to chip away tiles to get at plumbing, use a **cold chisel.**

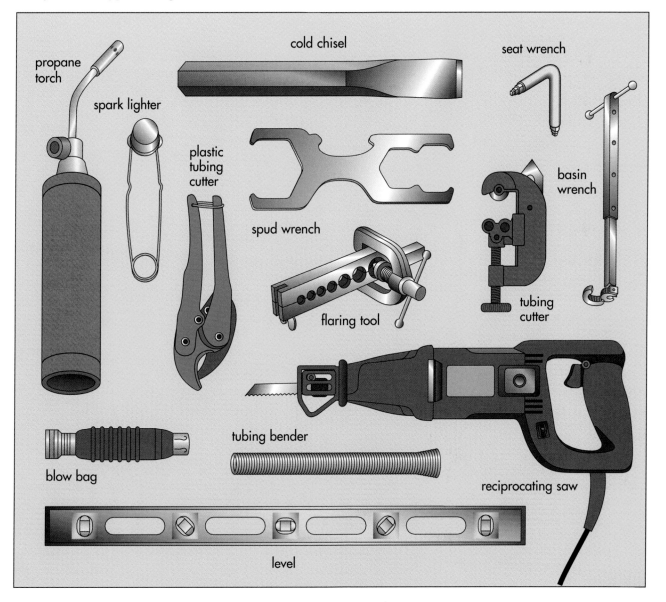

CHOOSING PIPE

The first step in choosing pipe is to find out which type of pipe you have in your home. It's often easiest to use the same type when adding on, but you don't have to continue using that type. To change type, you must purchase special adapter fittings to switch from one material to another in the middle of a pipe run.

For supply lines—the pipes that carry pressurized water to your fixtures—the usual choices are copper and plastic. However, if your home is old enough to have galvanized pipe and you need to install only a short run of pipe, it makes sense to continue with galvanized. In many localities, plastic supply pipe is not allowed.

Keep in mind that copper pipe will be difficult for you to install until you have spent time learning how to solder (see pages 18–19).

When making final connections to a fixture or a faucet, usually it is easiest to install a flexible supply line. Use copper or plastic flexible tubing. Be careful to avoid kinks.

Plastic pipe—either PVC or ABS—is now used almost exclusively for drains. If you have old cast-iron, galvanized, or copper drain pipes, make the transition to plastic. It is much easier to install and less expensive.

Before you buy any pipe, check with the local building department to make sure you're using material approved for use in your area.

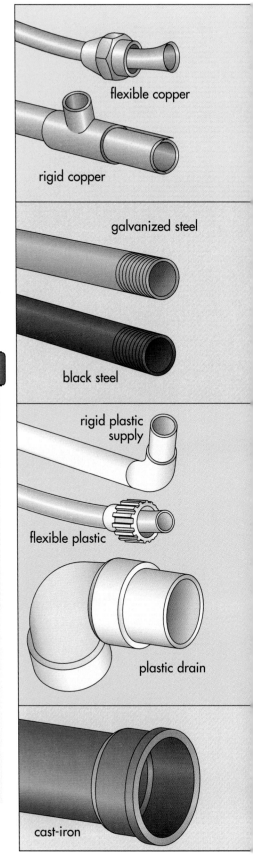

flexible copper

rigid copper

galvanized steel

black steel

rigid plastic supply

flexible plastic

plastic drain

cast-iron

EXPERTS' INSIGHT

GAS LINES

■ Gas lines are almost always made of black steel pipe. It has the same texture as galvanized pipe but not the shiny silver color. Black steel pipe is installed in the same way as galvanized pipe (see page 25). Check for leaks by turning the gas on, pouring soapy water on all the joints, and looking for tiny bubbles.

■ Contrary to some opinions, you can use galvanized pipe for gas, but it's more expensive. Do not use copper pipe for long gas lines. A chemical reaction causes the inside of the pipe to flake, which can plug orifices and damage appliances.

MEASUREMENTS

THE MOST COMMON SIZES

Here are the pipe sizes commonly used in residential plumbing in North America. (To determine the size of your pipe, see page 16.)

■ Main water-supply line entering a house: ¾–1 inch.

■ Water-supply lines after the water heater usually are ½ inch, sometimes ¾ inch.

■ Gas lines are most often ¾ inch and sometimes are ½ inch.

■ Main drain pipes, called stacks: 3 or 4 inches.

■ Kitchen, tub, and shower drains are almost always 1½ inches.

■ Bathroom sink drains are almost always 1¼ inches.

Material	Type	Uses	Features and Joining Techniques
Copper	Rigid	Hot and cold supply lines; rarely for DWV (drain-waste-vent) lines	Sold in 10' and 20' lengths. The most widely used pipe for supply lines. Lightweight and durable, though a bit expensive. Once the soldering technique is learned, you can cut it on the spot and put it together quickly. Type M is the thinnest, and is a good choice for home projects. Types L and K are used mainly in commercial projects.
	Flexible	Hot and cold supply lines, for short final runs to fixtures	Comes in easily bent 60' and 100' coils or by the foot. Can be soldered like rigid copper, but usually is connected with compression fittings.
Threaded Steel	Galvanized	Supply and occasionally DWV	Because it's cumbersome to work with and tends to build up lime deposits that constrict water flow, it is not used widely anymore. It takes expensive equipment to cut and thread it, so you must buy pre-cut pieces from your supplier. If you have a good selection of shorter pieces on hand, you can cut down on trips to the supplier.
	Black	Gas lines	Rusts readily, so it must not be used for water supply.
Plastic	ABS	DWV only	Black in color, in 10' or 20' lengths. Lightweight and easy to work with, you can cut it with an ordinary saw, and cement it together with a special glue. Check local codes before using.
	PVC	Cold water supply and DWV	Cream-colored, blue-gray, or white, in 10' or 20' lengths. This has the same properties as ABS, except that you must apply primer before cementing it. Do not mix PVC with ABS or interchange their cements.
	CPVC	Hot and cold supply lines	White, gray, or cream-colored, available in 10' lengths. Has the same properties as ABS and PVC.
	Flexible PB (polybutylene)	Hot and cold supply lines, usually for short runs	White or cream-colored, sold in 25' or 100' coils or by the foot. Flexible. Expensive and not widely used, it is joined with special fittings.
	Flexible PE (polyethylene)	Supply lines	Black-colored, sold in 25' or 100' coils or by the foot. Same properties as PB. Used for sprinkler systems.
Cast-Iron	Hub-and-Spigot	DWV	Cast-iron is extremely heavy and difficult to work with, so don't try to install any new pipes of this material. Hub-and-spigot is joined with oakum and molten lead.
	No-Hub	DWV	Joins with gaskets and clamps, but still is hard to work with. Make the transition to plastic instead.

CHOOSING THE RIGHT FITTING

The parts bins at a plumbing supplier contain hundreds of fittings that let you connect any pipe material in just about any way. To get the best pipe for your needs, familiarize yourself with the terms on this page. Items in bold are illustrated on pages 14–15.

Supply fittings connect the pipes that bring water to fixtures and faucets. When changing direction in a supply run, use an **elbow (ell)**. The most common ones make 90- or 45-degree turns and have female threads on each end. A **street ell** has male and female connections to allow for insertion into another fitting. A reducing ell joins one size pipe to another. Use a **drop ell** to anchor the pipes to framing where they will protrude into a room.

Use **tees** wherever two runs intersect. A **reducing tee** lets you join pipes of different diameters; for example, adding a ½-inch branch to a ¾-inch main supply.

A **coupling** connects pipes end to end. **Reducing couplings** let you step down from one pipe diameter to a smaller one. Slip couplings (see page 27) function the same way as unions, joining sections of copper or plastic line. Use a **cap** to seal off a line.

A plastic-to-copper **transition fitting** is one of many transition fittings that connect one pipe material to another. (Do not make the transition from steel to copper without a special dielectric fitting, or the joint will corrode.)

In any run of threaded pipe, you'll need a **union** somewhere. This fitting compensates for the frustrating fact that you can't simultaneously turn a pipe into fittings at either end.

Nipples—lengths of pipe less than 12 inches long—are sold in standard sizes because short pieces are difficult to cut and thread.

Examine drainage fittings, and you'll see how they're designed to keep waste water flowing downhill. Sometimes called **sanitary fittings**, they have gentle curves rather than sharp angles, so waste will not get hung up.

Choose ¼ **bends** to make 90-degree turns, and ⅛ **bends** for 45 degrees. Also available are ⅕ bends, for 72-degree turns, and ⅙ bends, for 60 degrees. All types of bends also come in more gradual curves, known as **long-turn bends**, which make for a smoother flow.

Sanitary branches such as the **tee** and **cross** shown here, come in a variety of configurations that suit situations where two or more lines converge. These can be tricky to order, so make a sketch of your proposed drain lines, identifying all pipe sizes, and take it to your supplier when you order.

Toilet hookups require a **closet bend,** which connects to the main drain, and a **closet flange**, which fits onto the bend. The flange is anchored to the floor and anchors the toilet bowl. To connect a sink trap to the drainpipe, use a **trap adapter.** To make the transition from cast-iron drain to plastic drain, use a **no-hub** adapter.

EXPERTS' INSIGHT

ORDERING OR FINDING FITTINGS

When ordering materials, organize your description of a fitting in this way: first the size, then the material, and finally the type of fitting. You might, for example, ask or look for a ½-inch galvanized, 90-degree ell. With reducing fittings, the larger size comes first, then the smaller.

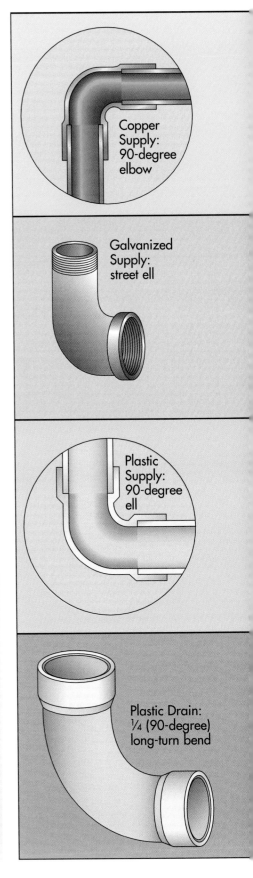

Copper Supply: 90-degree elbow

Galvanized Supply: street ell

Plastic Supply: 90-degree ell

Plastic Drain: ¼ (90-degree) long-turn bend

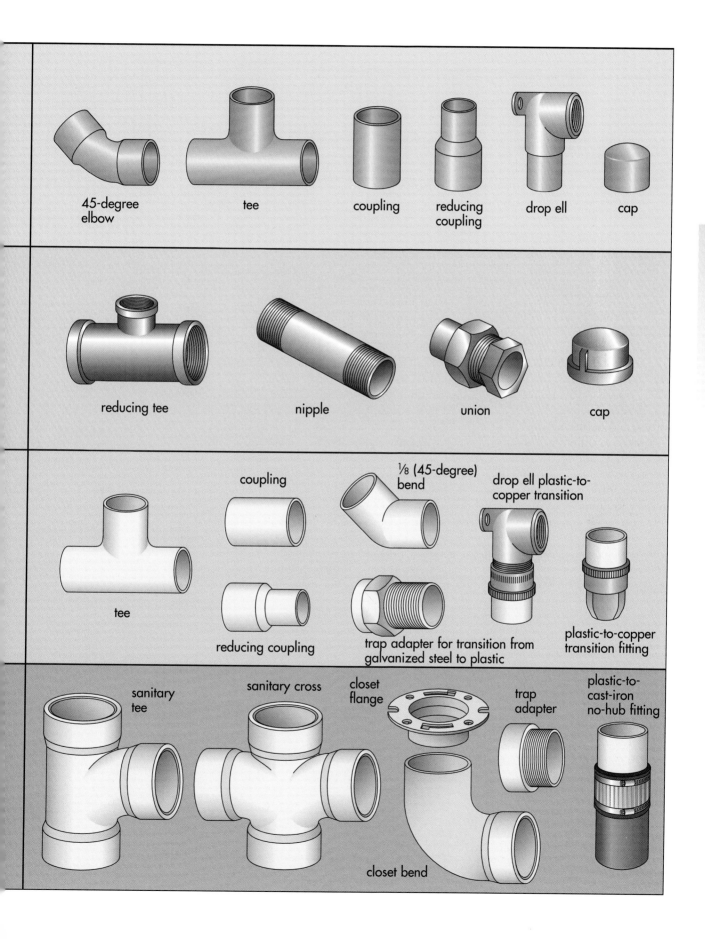

45-degree elbow

tee

coupling

reducing coupling

drop ell

cap

reducing tee

nipple

union

cap

tee

coupling

reducing coupling

⅛ (45-degree) bend

trap adapter for transition from galvanized steel to plastic

drop ell plastic-to-copper transition

plastic-to-copper transition fitting

sanitary tee

sanitary cross

closet flange

trap adapter

plastic-to-cast-iron no-hub fitting

closet bend

MEASURING PIPES AND FITTINGS

*B*eginning plumbers often spend more time running back and forth to their supplier than they spend doing the actual work because it takes practice and experience to be able to figure out everything you need ahead of time. The first step in becoming an efficient plumber is to learn to correctly identify the pipes and fittings a job requires.

Plumbing dimensions aren't always what they appear to be. A plastic pipe with a 7⁄8-inch outside diameter, for instance, is actually called a 1⁄2-inch pipe because it has a 1⁄2-inch inside diameter and pipes are usually sized according

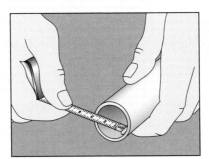

To find out a pipe's size, measure the inside ...

If you have a pipe with an exposed end, simply measure the pipe's inside diameter, and round off to the nearest 1⁄8 inch. Some manufacturers indicate the size on the fittings.

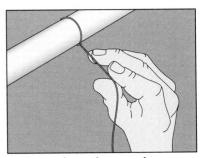

or figure from the outside.

You also can determine pipe size by measuring its outside circumference. Wrap a string around the pipe, straighten it out, and measure it. Use the chart below to find the nominal size you'll need to order.

MEASUREMENTS: PIPE DIMENSIONS

Material	Inside Diameter (ID) Nominal Size	Approximate Outside Diameter (OD)	Approximate Circumference	Approximate Socket Depth
Copper	1⁄4"	3⁄8"	1 1⁄8"	5⁄16"
	3⁄8"	1⁄2"	1 1⁄2"	3⁄8"
	1⁄2"	5⁄8"	2"	1⁄2"
	3⁄4"	7⁄8"	2 3⁄4"	3⁄4"
	1"	1 1⁄8"	3 1⁄2"	15⁄16"
	1 1⁄4"	1 3⁄8"	4 5⁄16"	1"
	1 1⁄2"	1 5⁄8"	5 1⁄8"	1 1⁄8"
Threaded	3⁄8"	5⁄8"	2"	3⁄8"
	1⁄2"	3⁄4"	2 3⁄8"	1⁄2"
	3⁄4"	1"	3 1⁄8"	9⁄16"
	1"	1 1⁄4"	4"	11⁄16"
	1 1⁄4"	1 1⁄2"	4 3⁄4"	11⁄16"
	1 1⁄2"	1 3⁄4"	5 1⁄2"	11⁄16"
	2"	2 1⁄4"	7"	3⁄4"
Plastic	1⁄2"	7⁄8"	2 3⁄4"	1⁄2"
	3⁄4"	1 1⁄8"	3 1⁄2"	5⁄8"
	1"	1 3⁄8"	4 5⁄16"	3⁄4"
	1 1⁄4"	1 5⁄8"	5 1⁄8"	11⁄16"
	1 1⁄2"	1 7⁄8"	6"	11⁄16"
	2"	2 3⁄8"	7 1⁄2"	3⁄4"
	3"	3 3⁄8"	10 1⁄2"	1 1⁄2"
	4"	4 3⁄8"	14"	1 3⁄4"
Cast-Iron	2"	2 1⁄4"	7"	2 1⁄2"
	3"	3 1⁄4"	10 1⁄8"	2 3⁄4"
	4"	4 1⁄4"	13 3⁄8"	3"

to their inside diameter (ID). (See chart on page 16.) This dimension is also referred to as the nominal size, the size you ask for at a plumbing supplier.

If you are at all unsure about getting the right material, make things perfectly clear by specifying ID for most pipes. In a minority of cases—flexible copper lines, for example—pipe is ordered by using the outside diameter (OD).

If you can measure the inside dimension, you're home free. However, often you won't have a way of measuring the inside of the pipe. Holding a ruler against a pipe will give you only a rough idea of the outside diameter. Instead, use a string or a set of calipers for a more exact measurement. Once you find the outside dimension, use the chart, opposite, to find the nominal size.

Fittings can be just as confusing. Their inside diameters must be large enough to fit over the pipe's outside diameter so that a half-inch plastic elbow, for example, has an outside diameter of about 1¼ inches.

As a rule of thumb, the OD of copper is ⅛ inch greater than its ID, the nominal size. For plastic pipe, measure the OD and subtract ⅜ inch. For threaded and cast-iron, subtract ¼ inch.

Another mathematical pitfall for a beginning plumber is measuring the length of a pipe running from one fitting to the next. Pipes must fully extend into fixture and fitting sockets (see illustration, right), or the joint could leak. Socket depths vary from one pipe size and material to another, so you must account for the depth of each fitting's socket in the total length of pipe needed between fittings.

The only times you don't have to take socket depth into account are when you are using no-hub cast-iron pipes (see page 87) or slip couplings with copper or plastic pipe (see page 33).

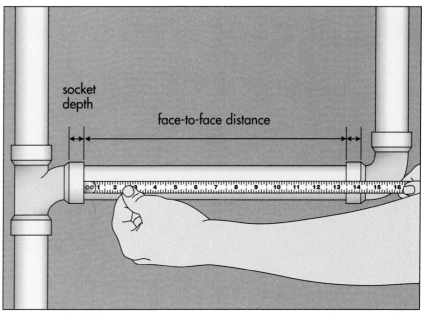

socket depth

face-to-face distance

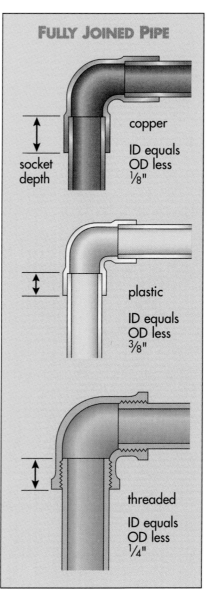

FULLY JOINED PIPE

socket depth

copper

ID equals OD less ⅛"

plastic

ID equals OD less ⅜"

threaded

ID equals OD less ¼"

Add the socket depths.
To figure the length of a pipe, first measure from face to face, as shown above. Next, check the chart on page 16 for the socket depth of the material you're working with. Because pipes have fittings on both ends, multiply by 2, and add the face-to-face length.

Measure copper or plastic in place.
When working with copper or plastic—materials you can cut on the job—often the most accurate way of measuring is to insert the pipe into one fitting and mark the other end, rather than using a tape measure.

EXPERTS' INSIGHT

Don't leave the household high and dry while you drive back and forth to the plumbing supplier. When buying fittings, invest in a handful of caps in different sizes. That way, if you've misread a dimension—as even experienced plumbers do occasionally—you can easily cap off the line and turn the water on again.

WORKING WITH RIGID COPPER PIPE

*T*o solder rigid copper plumbing lines, you must learn a skill that is unlike other household repair skills. At first, it may seem frustratingly slow. But once you get the knack, soldering will go faster than screwing together threaded pipe.

Sometimes soldering is called "sweating." Soldering works by using capillary action to flow molten solder into the fitting. Just as an ink blotter soaks up ink, a joint absorbs molten solder, making a watertight bond as strong as the pipe itself.

YOU'LL NEED...

TIME: With practice, an hour to connect five joints.
SKILLS: Soldering is a specialized skill that takes time to learn.
MATERIALS: Pipe, lead-free solder.
TOOLS: Tubing cutter or hacksaw, emery cloth, wire brush, flux brush, propane torch, tongue-and-groove pliers.

EXPERTS' INSIGHT

ELIMINATING MOISTURE

If you are adding on to existing plumbing, there may be a little water inside the pipes. This must be dried up if you are to solder a tight joint.

■ Stuff in a piece of white bread (not the crust) just upstream of the connection. It will absorb the water, and dissolve when the water is turned on.

■ Buy specially made waxy capsules that plug the line while you work. Later, apply heat where the capsule lodged to melt the capsule away.

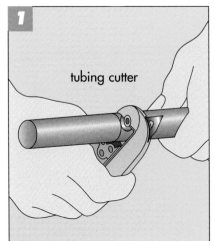

1. Cut the pipe.
Use a tubing cutter or a hacksaw. A tubing cutter makes cleaner cuts. Clamp the cutter onto the tubing, rotate a few revolutions, tighten, and rotate some more. Make hacksaw cuts in a miter box. Don't nick the metal—this could cause the connection to leak.

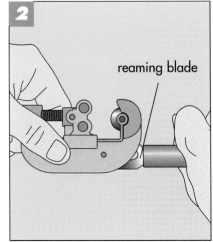

2. Remove burrs.
Remove any burrs on the inside of the pipe by inserting the reaming blade of the tubing cutter and twisting. If you don't have a tubing cutter, use a metal file.

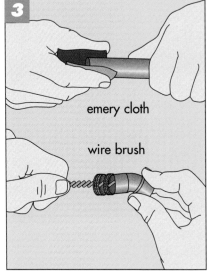

3. Polish the pipe and fitting.
Polish the outside of the pipe and the inside of the fitting with emery cloth or steel wool. This removes grease, dirt, and oxidation that could impede the flow of solder. Stop polishing when the metal is shiny. Avoid touching polished surfaces—oil from your fingers could interfere with the solder flow and cause a leak.

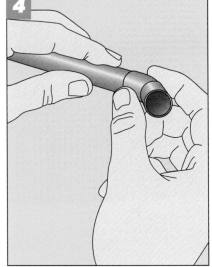

4. Dry-fit the pieces.
Dry-fit a number of pipe pieces and fittings to make sure they are the right length. If you have difficulty pushing pieces together, the pipe may have been squeezed out of shape during cutting. Cut a new piece. Once you are satisfied, take them apart and set them on a clean surface.

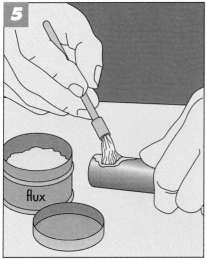

5. Apply flux.

Brush on a light, even coating of flux (also called soldering paste) to both surfaces. Flux retards oxidation when the copper is heated. As solder flows into the joint, the flux burns away. Use rosin- (not acid-) type flux for plumbing work.

6. Protect flammable surfaces.

If you're working near framing, paper-sheathed insulation, or other flammable materials, shield them from the propane torch flame with an old cookie sheet or a piece of sheet metal.

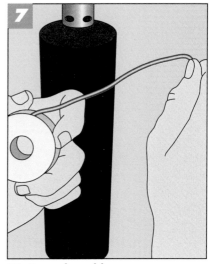

7. Form the solder.

Bend the solder so it's easy to work with but long enough to keep your fingers away from the flame. Unwind about 10 inches of solder, straighten it, and bend 2 inches at a 60-degree angle. Light the torch. Adjust the flame until the inner (blue) cone is about 2 inches long.

8. Assemble the connection.

Heat the middle of the fitting—not the joint—with the inner cone of the flame. Touch the solder to the joint. If it is hot enough, capillary action will pull solder into the joint. Remove the flame when solder drips from the pipe.

CAUTION!
Any gaps will leak. Be sure the joint has an even bead around its circumference to prevent leaks.

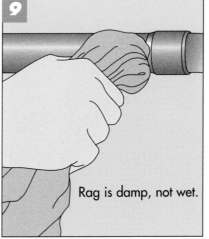

9. Wipe away excess.

For a neat, professional look, lightly brush the joint with a damp rag. Take care not to burn your fingers.

Most pros lay out an entire run of copper, first cutting and dry-fitting all of its components. After dry-fitting, they go back to clean, flux, and solder each joint.

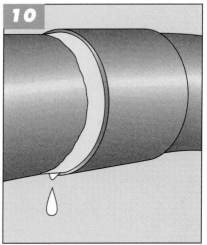

10. Check for leaks.

Test the system by turning the water on. If you have a leak, there is no easy solution—it cannot be fixed while water is present. Shut off the water, drain the line, disassemble the joint (see page 20), and discard the old fitting. Dry the inside of the pipes. Polish the pipe end and the inside of the new fitting, apply flux, reassemble, and solder again.

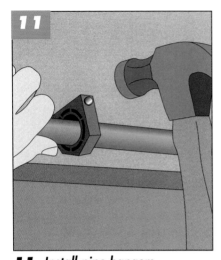

11. Install pipe hangers.
Copper supply lines need support at least every 6 feet. The plastic type of hanger pictured here is easy to install, helps quiet noisy pipes, and is slightly flexible so it doesn't damage the pipes.

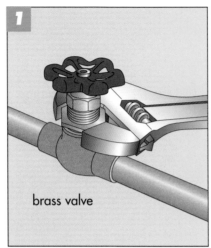

1. To install a brass valve, remove any heat-sensitive parts.
A valve stem has rubber or plastic parts that will melt during soldering. Remove the stem with a wrench. Polish the pipe end and the inside of the fitting as you would with a copper joint.

brass valve

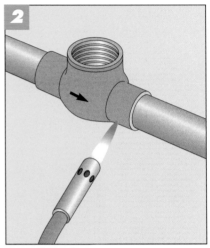

2. Solder the joint.
Fit the pieces together. (If the valve has an arrow, be sure it is pointing in the direction of water flow). Heat the body of the valve, moving the flame back and forth to heat both sides evenly. Brass requires more heating than copper. Apply solder as you would with a copper fitting (see page 19).

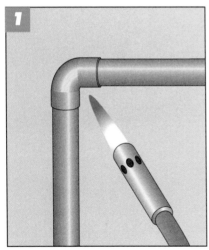

1. To take apart soldered joints, heat the fitting.
NOTE: *Shut off the water.* Drain the line by opening faucets above and below the run. Light a propane torch, set it so the inner (blue) cone of the flame is about 2 inches long, and heat the fitting. Point the flame at both sides of the fitting, but not directly at the soldered joint.

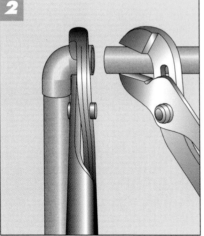

2. Pull the pieces apart.
While the pipe is hot, grasp the fitting and pipe with pliers, and pull the joint apart.

> **CAUTION!**
> *Once the fitting is heated, you have only a few seconds to take the joint apart. Prepare a safe place to set the torch and have two pairs of pliers within easy reach. Work carefully—the pipes are very hot.*

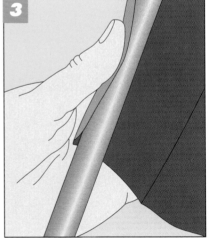

3. Polish the pipe ends.
To remove old solder, heat the pipe end with the torch, and quickly wipe with a dry rag. Do this carefully—the pipe is very hot. Allow the pipe to cool, and polish the end with emery cloth. Never reuse old copper fittings—a watertight seal can only be made with a new fitting.

WORKING WITH FLEXIBLE COPPER TUBING

Flexible copper tubing is pliable enough to make all but the sharpest turns. This means you don't have to install a fitting every time you make a turn as you would with rigid pipe. In almost every case, you should connect flexible tubing to compression and flare fittings (see pages 22–23) rather than soldering them.

Do not use copper tubing for a gas line. Natural gas will cause the inside of the copper tube to flake, which can damage appliances.

YOU'LL NEED...
TIME: To bend and cut tubing for a short run, about 15 minutes.
SKILLS: Patience and care to keep from kinking tubing.
TOOLS: Tubing cutter, coil-spring tubing bender.

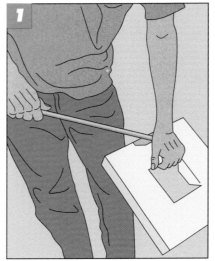

1. Uncoil the tubing.
Because flexible copper tubing is soft, always handle it gently. Uncoil tubing by straightening it out every few inches as you go. If the tubing comes in a box, grip the box, and carefully pull the tubing upward.

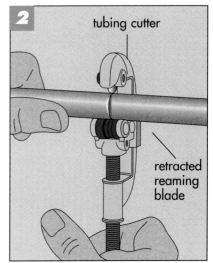

2. Cut the tubing.
Cut flexible tubing with a tubing cutter or a hacksaw. Remove any burrs on the inside of the tubing by inserting the reaming blade of the tubing cutter and twisting. Or, use a metal file.

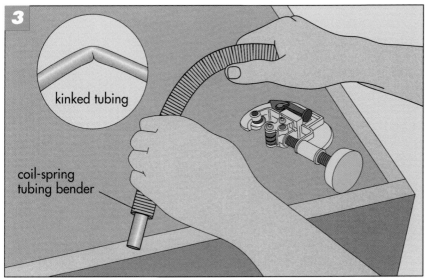

kinked tubing

coil-spring tubing bender

3. Bend the tubing.
Bend the flexible tubing in gradual, sweeping arcs, or it will surprise you by suddenly kinking, and you'll have to throw the piece away. Kinks seriously impede water flow and are almost impossible to reshape.

If you need to make a fairly tight turn, use a coil-spring tubing bender like the one shown here. Slide the bender to the point you need a tight bend and, with it in place, bend the tubing. With one of these tools, it is nearly impossible to kink the tubing.

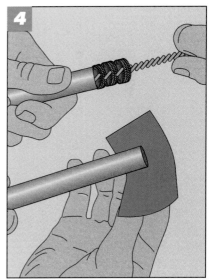

4. Polish the end.
Rub the end of the tubing lightly with emery cloth to remove dirt and grease. With compression or flare fittings, you don't need to polish as much as for a soldered joint. Join tubing by using compression fittings (see page 22) or flare fittings (see page 23), or by soldering (see pages 18–19).

USING COMPRESSION FITTINGS

Use compression fittings in places where you may need to take the run apart someday or where it is difficult to solder. One common location is on supply lines for a sink, which have compression fittings at both the stop valve and the faucet inlet. Flexible supply lines are an even easier way to make this connection (see page 49).

Compression fittings usually are used with flexible copper tubing, but may also be used with type-M rigid copper (see page 12). These fittings are not as strong as soldered joints, so they should not be hidden inside walls.

YOU'LL NEED...

TIME: About 15 minutes to make a simple connection.
SKILLS: No special skills needed.
TOOLS: Two Crescent wrenches.

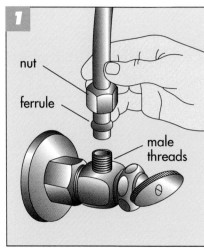

1. To make a compression joint, position the parts.
Bend the tubing into position (see page 21), and slip on the nut and the ferrule. The ferrule will not go on if the tubing end is bent or less than perfectly round. You may have to sand it with emery cloth to get it to slide on. Smear pipe joint compound on the ferrule and the male threads of the fitting.

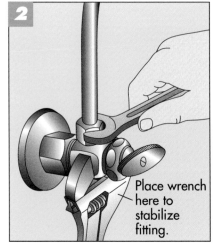

Place wrench here to stabilize fitting.

2. Tighten the nut.
Tighten the compression nut with a wrench, forcing the ferrule down into the tubing to secure and seal the connection. If the joint leaks when the water is turned on, tighten the nut a quarter turn at a time until the leak stops. Don't overtighten the joint—too much pressure can crush the tubing or crack the nut.

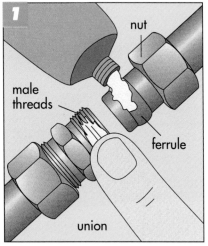

1. To join a compression union, position the parts.
Bend the tubing pieces into position (see page 21), and slip a nut and a ferrule onto each piece of tubing. Smear pipe joint compound on the ferrules and on the male threads of the union. Slide the pieces together, and hand-tighten the nuts.

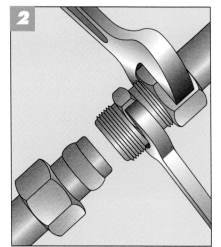

2. Tighten each side.
Place one wrench on the union. Use another wrench to tighten each side. Once snug, tighten about a half turn more. Turn on the water, and, if there is a leak, gently tighten more.

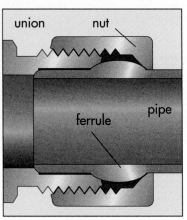

How it works
The compression nut forms a seal by squeezing the ferrule against the copper pipe. Because copper is a soft metal, the seal can be extremely tight. Still, use pipe joint compound to make sure the seal is watertight. Anchor or support the tubing within 2 feet of either side of the fitting.

USING FLARE FITTINGS

Flare fittings, like compression fittings, are useful in places where it's difficult to solder a joint. Do not hide flare fittings inside a wall. You can use flare fittings only with flexible copper tubing; they cannot be used on rigid pipe. Unlike compression fittings, this type of fitting requires a flaring tool. The two-piece tool reshapes the end of the copper tubing, "flaring" it to fit into a special flare fitting. If possible, make the flared connection first, then cut the tubing to length because sometimes tubing splits while being flared.

YOU'LL NEED...

TIME: About half an hour to join two pieces together in a union.
SKILLS: Use of the flaring tool is not difficult.
TOOLS: Flaring tool, adjustable wrenches.

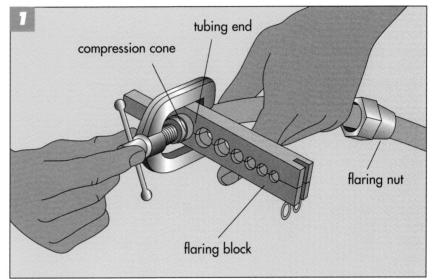

1. Flare the tubing ends.
The first thing to remember: Slip the flaring nut on before you flare the end of the tubing.

Choose the hole in the flaring block that matches the outside diameter of the tubing. Clamp the tool onto the tubing. Align the compression cone on the tubing's end, and tighten the screw. As you turn the handle, the cone flares the tubing's end. Inspect your work carefully after removing the tubing from the block. If the end has split, cut off the flared portion and repeat the process.

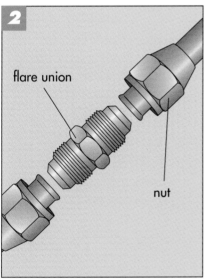

2. Assemble the pieces.
Seat the flare union against one of the flared ends of the tubing, slide the nut down, and hand-tighten. Do the same on the other side. No pipe joint compound is necessary.

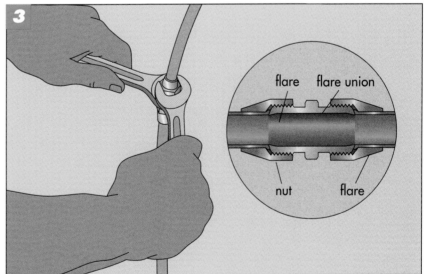

3. Tighten and test.
Place one wrench on the union and one on a nut. Don't over-tighten a flared joint. Once snug, give it a half turn on each nut. Turn the water on and test. If the joint leaks, tighten it carefully until the leak stops. If tightening won't stop the leak, dismantle the joint and examine it to see if the tubing was cut squarely. Make sure that the nut was not cross-threaded on the fitting. Anchor or support the tubing within 2 feet of either side of the flare fitting.

REMOVING OLD THREADED PIPE

After your first experience with threaded pipe, you'll appreciate why this material is all but extinct in new installations. Cutting, threading, and assembling steel pipe requires muscle. Sometimes when you're trying to take old pipe apart, you'll swear it is welded together.

If your home was built before World War II, its supply pipes are likely to be threaded steel. This doesn't mean you have to use the same pipe for improvements or repairs. Special fittings let you break into a line and add copper or plastic (see pages 14–15).

Black threaded pipe, which lacks the shiny gray color of galvanized, is meant for gas only, and is still commonly used. Do not use black pipe for water lines.

YOU'LL NEED...

TIME: To take apart four or five sections of pipe with fittings, about an hour.
SKILLS: Use of a pipe wrench and sometimes brute strength.
TOOLS: Two pipe wrenches, hacksaw, maybe a propane torch.

EXPERTS' INSIGHT

SWITCHING MATERIALS

If you have good water pressure and can find no serious rust, there is no need to replace your threaded steel pipe with copper or plastic. But if water pressure is low, aerators fill up with rust, and leaks develop, it is time for a change. Replace the worst-looking pipes first. Don't cut holes into walls and get involved in a major refit unless it is absolutely necessary.

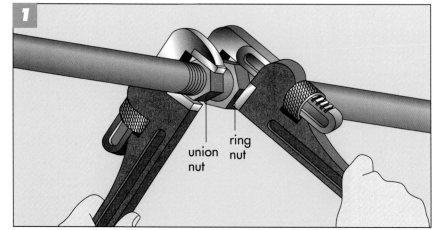

1. Start at a union.
NOTE: *Shut off water, and drain the pipes.* Examine the way your pipes and fittings thread together and you'll see you can't simply begin unscrewing them anywhere. Somewhere in every pipe run is a union that allows you to unlock and dismantle the piping. To crack open a union, determine which of the smaller union nuts the ring nut is threaded onto. With one wrench on each, turn the ring nut counterclockwise. Once it's unthreaded, you have the break you need and can start unscrewing pipes from fittings. When unscrewing pipe, use the second wrench to keep the fitting from turning while you unscrew.

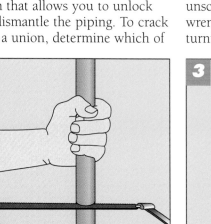

2. When necessary, cut the pipe.
If there is no union handy, cut a pipe with a hacksaw or a reciprocating saw fitted with a metal-cutting blade. When you reassemble the run, you'll probably have to install a union using prethreaded nipples on either side of the union.

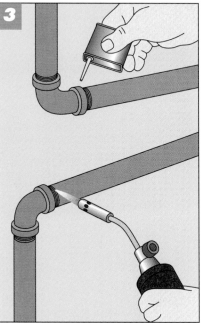

3. If the pipe won't budge
Stubborn joints may respond to penetrating oil, or try heating the fitting with a propane torch. Then use a larger pipe wrench, or slip a piece of 1¼-inch or 1½-inch pipe onto the handle of your wrench to increase its leverage.

INSTALLING THREADED PIPE

If you choose to work with threaded pipe, one difficulty is ending the run at the right place. Because the ends of the pipe are threaded, you can't just cut a piece to fit, as with copper or plastic. Purchase long pieces that take up most of the runs, and have on hand plenty of couplings and a selection of nipples, or short lengths of pipe that are threaded on each end. You will then have a number of options to choose from to end the run in the right spot.

YOU'LL NEED...

TIME: In an hour you can assemble about four pipe lengths with fittings.
SKILLS: Pipe measuring, use of pipe wrench.
TOOLS: Tape measure, two pipe wrenches.

EXPERTS' INSIGHT

BOOSTING PRESSURE

■ Poor water pressure in an old house may be due to galvanized pipes that are clogged with rust. If the problem is limited to one fixture, try replacing a few of the pipes leading up to it. If the problem is throughout your house, call in a professional.

■ In many localities there are companies that specialize in unclogging galvanized pipe. They use a process that causes rust and corrosion to fall away from the inside of the pipe. The process can take months, will clog faucets, and may reveal leaks as gunk plugging holes is removed. In the end, however, water will flow through your pipes as if they were new.

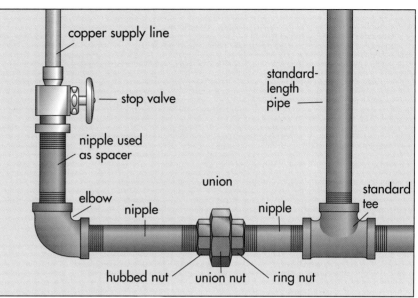

Assembling the parts

This typical installation combines standard-length pipes with joints and nipples to end up exactly at the right location. (For background on measuring pipe accurately, see pages 16–17.) Many plumbing suppliers have ready-cut galvanized pipe in standard sizes—12 inches, 48 inches, and so on—for less cost and delay than having pieces custom-cut. Try to use these pieces; if you make a mistake in measuring, you may not be allowed to return a custom-cut piece.

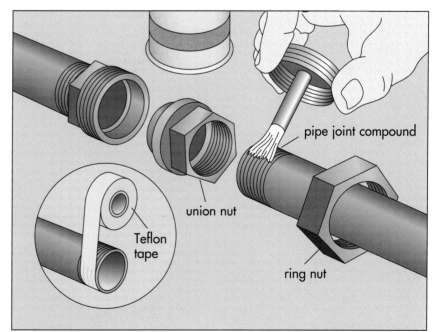

Joining the pieces

Before you thread a pipe and fitting together, seal the pipe threads using pipe joint compound or Teflon tape. Assemble the pipes and fittings one at a time, tightening each as you go. If your assembly requires a union, work from each end toward the union. The union is installed last. Support runs of threaded pipe at least every 6 feet.

WORKING WITH RIGID PLASTIC PIPE

Plastic plumbing is popular with do-it-yourselfers because it is inexpensive and easy to work with. Plastic pipe cuts with an ordinary hacksaw, and goes together without special tools or techniques. You simply clean the burrs from the cut, prime, and glue the parts together.

Still, installing plastic pipe requires attention to detail, planning ahead, and doing things in the right order. If you make a mistake, the parts cannot be disassembled. You'll have to cut out the faulty section, throw it out, and start again.

There are various types of plastic, so check local codes to make sure you are using the right type for your purpose. In most localities, either ABS or PVC are accepted (sometimes even required) for drain lines. Many localities do not accept plastic pipe for supply lines; others specify CPVC. See pages 12–13 for types of plastic pipe. Do not mix ABS with PVC. Each expands at a different rate, and each uses a differently formulated cement. Plastic pipe is not as stiff as metal. Be sure to support horizontal runs every 4 to 5 feet.

YOU'LL NEED...

TIME: With practice, you can cut and install about five fittings and five pieces of pipe in an hour.
SKILLS: Measuring, cutting, and assembling components in a logical manner.
TOOLS: Plastic pipe saw or hacksaw, miter box, tape measure, utility knife, pencil, emery cloth, plastic tubing cutter for supply lines.

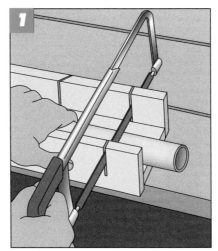

1. Measure and cut.
When measuring pipe for cutting, take the socket depth of the fitting into account (see pages 16–17). Cut with any fine-tooth saw, using a miter box. Avoid diagonal cuts because they reduce the bonding area at the deepest part of the fitting's socket—the most critical part of the joint.

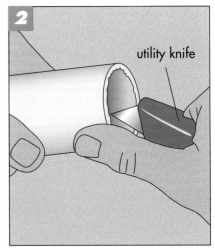

2. Remove burrs from the cut end.
After you've made the cut, use a knife or file to remove any burrs from the inside and outside of the cut end. Burrs can scrape away cement when the pipe is pushed into the fitting, seriously weakening the bond.

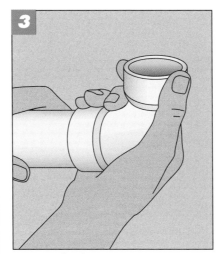

3. Test the fitting.
Dry-fit the connection. You should be able to push it in at least one-third of the way. If the pipe bottoms out and feels loose, try another fitting. Unlike copper components, plastic systems are designed with tapered walls on the inside of the socket so that the pipe makes contact well before the pipe reaches the socket shoulder.

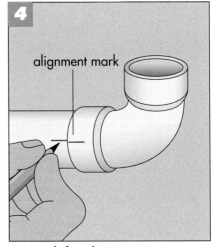

4. Mark for alignment.
When gluing the pieces together, you will have less than a minute to correctly position the pipe and fitting before the glue sets. Draw an alignment mark across the pipe and fitting of each joint. When you fit the pieces together, the mark will indicate exactly how to position the pipe and fitting.

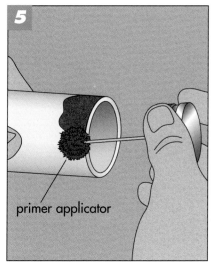

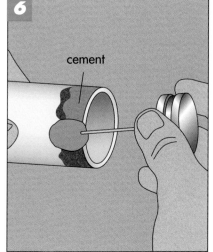

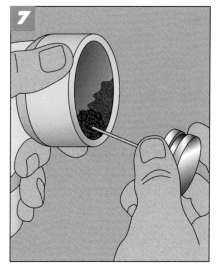

5. Clean and prime.

Wipe the inside of the fitting and the outside of the pipe end with a clean cloth. If you are working with PVC or CPVC (but not ABS), coat the outside of the pipe end with a special primer. Many inspectors require purple-colored primer so they can easily see that joints have been primed.

6. Apply cement to pipe.

Use the cement designed for the material you're working with. Immediately after you've primed, swab a smooth coating of cement onto the pipe end.

7. Prime and cement fitting.

Repeat the process on the inside of the fitting socket. Apply cement liberally, but don't let it puddle inside the fitting. Reapply a coating of cement to the pipe end.

EXPERTS' INSIGHT

DRY-FIT 3 OR 4 PIECES AHEAD

Whenever possible, cut and dry-fit three or four pieces before priming and gluing. That way, you can get things lined up ahead of time and avoid going back and forth between cans of primer and cement.

However, don't dry-fit more than four pieces, and don't dry-fit an entire section that must come out to an exact length. Plastic is not like copper pipe, which will solder together exactly the way it dry-fit. Once the cement is applied, plastic pipes may slide farther in than they did during the dry run, which can throw your measurements off as much as ¼ inch per fitting.

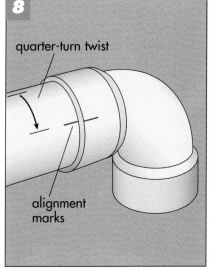

8. Twist and hold.

Forcefully push the two together to ensure the pipe moves fully into the socket. Twist a quarter turn as you push to help spread the cement evenly. Complete the twist until your alignment marks come together. Hold the pipe and fitting together for about 20 seconds while they fuse into a single piece. Wipe away excess cement.

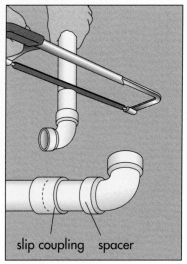

Cut off any incorrect joints.

If you misalign a connection, saw it off, making sure to cut squarely. Install a new fitting with a spacer and slip coupling as shown. Cemented joints are strong enough to handle after 15 minutes, but don't run water in the line for about two hours.

WORKING WITH FLEXIBLE PLASTIC TUBING

Like flexible copper tubing, flexible plastic tubing comes in long coils that you can snake through tight spots without using fittings. It kinks if bent too far, but doesn't kink as readily as flexible copper tubing. Codes in your area may disallow it entirely. If they do allow it, they will specify which type can be used in specific situations. PB (polybutylene) flexible plastic tubing can be used for hot and cold lines. Less expensive PE (polyethylene) tubing is affected by heat and therefore can be used to carry cold water only. Many communities allow its use underground for wells and sprinkler systems.

Both types of tubing are easy to work with: Cut the tubing with a knife, and join sections with clamps or compression fittings. Connect flexible plastic to other pipe materials with transition fittings that allow expansion and contraction. Support tubing every 32 inches, and clamp it loosely. PE and PB can be punctured, so don't use either for exposed runs.

YOU'LL NEED...

TIME: About two hours to connect three lengths.
SKILLS: No special skills needed.
TOOLS: Utility knife, pliers, screwdriver.

TOOLS TO USE

PLASTIC TUBING CUTTER

If you have a lot of tubing to cut (as you will if you are installing a sprinkler system), buy a plastic tubing cutter. With this tool, you can snip the tubing easily.

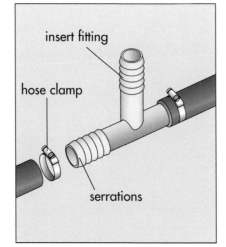

Connect PE flexible tubing with inserts and clamps.
Use insert fittings to connect PE tubing. Slip hose clamps over the ends of the tubing, push the tubing onto the insert, and tighten the clamp. Check that the serrations of the fittings are fully inserted in the tubing. The hose clamp should be positioned squarely on the serrations.

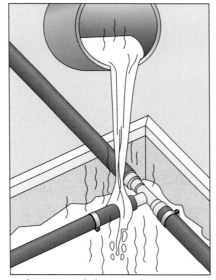

Soften PE with hot water.
Sometimes it takes a lot of muscle to push PE tubing over an insert fitting. Soak the tubing in hot water, or pour hot water over the tubing to soften it so it slips on easily. Use the same technique to dismantle a stubborn connection.

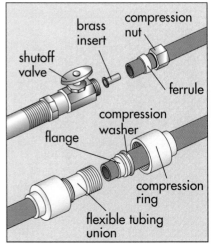

For PB flexible tubing, use compression fittings.
Attach PB to a metal stop valve with a compression nut and ferrule. A brass insert keeps the tubing from collapsing as the nut is tightened. A flexible tubing union joins two sections of tubing. Such a union should be tightened only by hand. You also can buy tees, ells, and other supply fittings.

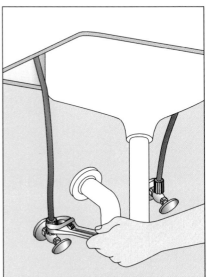

Use flexible plastic supplies.
PB makes an excellent choice for stop-to-fixture hookups, allowing you a margin of error during installation. Avoid bending it excessively, or it may kink. Don't overtighten the nuts.

QUIETING NOISY PIPES

Sudden changes in water pressure can vibrate pipes, causing noise when the pipes hit the house's framing. This page tells you what causes the noise and what you can do about it.

First identify the type of noise and its cause. Water hammer is the most common pipe noise. It results from a sudden stop in the flow of water, as when you turn off a faucet. The abrupt halting of water flow creates a shock wave in the pipes, causing them to vibrate and hit against framing members.

A ticking noise can be traced to a hot water pipe that was cool, then suddenly is heated by water running through it. Pipe insulation dampens the noise. Chattering or moaning sounds may be caused by water pressure that is too high. If this is a persistent problem, call a professional to check the pressure.

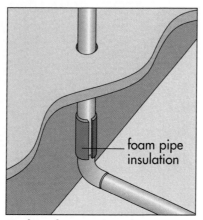

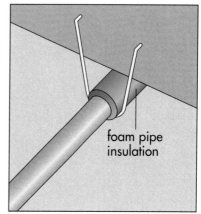

Cushion hammering pipes.
Have a helper do whatever it is that causes the noise while you search for the source of the noise. Once you find the source, check to see if one of the pipes has been knocking up against or rubbing a joist. Cushion the pipe at the trouble spot with pieces of foam pipe insulation, or use sound-insulating pipe hangers.

<table>
<tr><td>

YOU'LL NEED...
TIME: Several hours to install an air chamber or cushion pipes.
SKILLS: Connecting pipes.
TOOLS: Knife and hammer for pipe insulation; basic plumbing tools for adding an air chamber.

</td></tr>
</table>

EXPERTS' INSIGHT

DON'T BLAME PIPES
■ A machine-gun rattle, that annoying sound sometimes heard when you barely open a faucet, usually is caused by a defective seat washer.
■ Do pipes pound only when the dishwasher is running? An aging pump valve creates the same effect as a defective seat washer. Replace the pump.

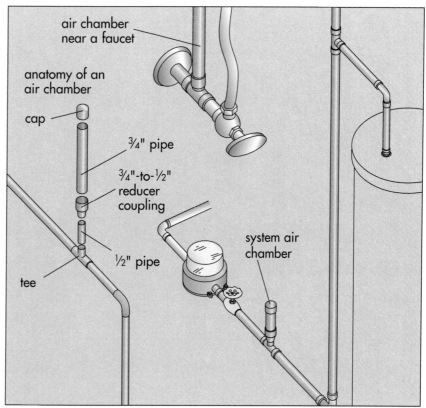

Install an air chamber.
To eliminate pipe noises, install air chambers at accessible points in your supply lines. These provide a pocket of air for water to bump against. Cut the pipe, install a tee (see pages 18–19), and solder the chamber in place. For galvanized pipe, cut the pipe and with nipples and a union, install a tee to which the chamber can be attached (see pages 24–25).

INSTALLING STOP VALVES

A ny time a water line bursts, a faucet needs repair, or a toilet needs replacing, you'll be grateful to have a stop valve in the right place. Without one of these handy devices, you may have to shut off the water to the entire house simply to change a faucet washer. If you have an older home that lacks stop valves under sinks and toilets, plan to install them.

No matter what the material or size of your pipes, there's a stop valve made to order. With copper lines, use brass valves. Galvanized and plastic pipes take steel and plastic stop valves respectively. You can also use a transition fitting (see page 15) to change material just prior to the stop. If the valve will be in view, choose a chrome finish.

To make the connection from a stop valve to a sink or toilet, you can use flexible copper or plastic line. Or throw away the nut and ferrule that come with the valve, and use the handy plastic or braided-metal flexible supply lines that simply screw on.

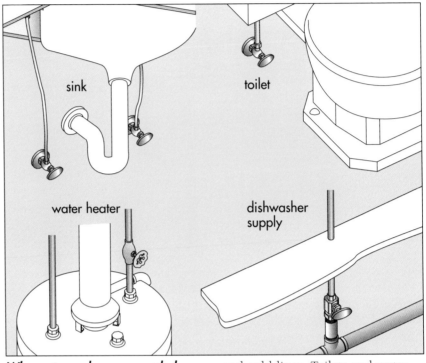

Where stop valves are needed
To determine your stop valve needs, simply take a look at your home's plumbing fixtures. Sinks, tubs, showers, and clothes washers should have one on both the hot and cold lines. Toilets and water heaters require only one, on the cold water line, and dishwashers need one on the hot line only. Check the water meter, too. It should have a valve just beyond it.

YOU'LL NEED...
TIME: About two hours to cut a pipe, install a stop valve, and run flexible line to the fixture.
SKILLS: Cutting, connecting pipe.
TOOLS: Hacksaw, tongue-and-groove pliers, tubing cutter, Crescent wrench, propane torch (for copper).

MEASUREMENTS

MATCH THE VALVE WITH THE FLEXIBLE LINE
Stop valves for sinks and toilets come with either ½- or ⅜-inch outlets. Make sure your flexible line is the same size.

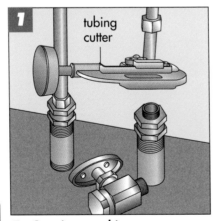

1. Cut pipe or tubing.
In the example shown, the existing plumbing consists of galvanized pipe and flexible copper tubing. To make room for the stop valve, cut enough tubing off to make room for the valve. Leave enough supply to fit the compression fitting and allow for tightening the stop valve on the steel pipe.

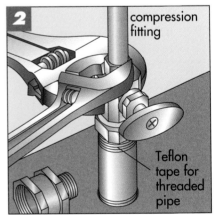

2. Install the valve.
One end of the stop valve is sized to fit regular pipe, and the other receives compression-fitted flexible lines. Wrap the galvanized pipe clockwise with Teflon tape, and install the stop valve. Slip the copper line into the other end, and tighten the compression fitting, holding the stop valve in place with a second wrench.

TROUBLESHOOTING MAIN LINE VALVES

In an older home, the shutoff valves for your main line may be worn and rusted. If you have a shutoff up-line from the valve, you can easily shut off the water and replace the valve. But often there is none, so you may have to live with a less-than-perfect valve rather than paying the water company to shut off your water while you change valves.

If the shutoff valve handle breaks off in such a way that you cannot simply replace it, use pliers or a pipe wrench for those few times when you need to use the valve. However, to make sure all household members can turn off the water in case of an emergency, replace the valve.

Another common problem is a slight leak from the packing nut when the valve is opened or closed. When this happens, try tightening the nut gently. Don't apply too much force when tightening, or the valve may crack. If you still have a slow drip, place a bucket under it, and watch it for a day or two—sometimes the leak will stop on its own.

If it doesn't, you will need to repack the valve. Make sure the valve is shut off—turn it clockwise until it tightens. Unscrew the screw at the top, and remove the handle. Loosen and remove the packing nut. Apply strand packing or a packing washer (see page 38), and reinstall the packing nut.

You can purchase valves that screw onto galvanized pipe or brass adapters, or solder-on types for copper lines.

YOU'LL NEED...

TIME: About an hour.
SKILLS: No special skills needed.
TOOLS: Screwdriver, Crescent wrench, tongue-and-groove pliers, pipe wrench.

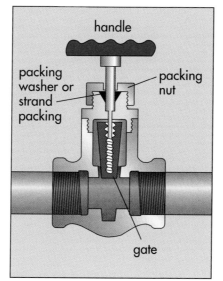

Gate valve
This older style of valve, commonly found in older houses, is not as reliable as a globe or ball valve, so replace it if you have the opportunity. A wedge-shaped brass "gate" screws up and down to control water flow. If it does not fully stop water flow, it cannot be repaired. Repair a leak around the handle by replacing the packing washer or strand packing.

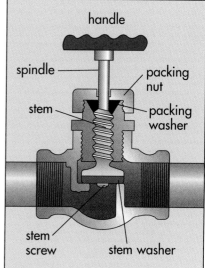

Globe valve
This works in much the same way as stem faucets (see page 36). It is more reliable and more easily repaired than a gate valve. If it does not fully stop water, and if you can shut off the flow prior to the valve, replace the stem washer. Repair a leak around the handle by replacing the packing washer.

EXPERTS' INSIGHT

AVOID CLOGGING FAUCETS

Over the years, old pipes build up rust, lime, and sediment deposits. Whenever you shut off water and turn it back on in a house with old galvanized pipe, you will cause these deposits to loosen and flow through the pipes. After turning off the main valve, take the time to remove aerators from the faucets, and let the water run for a couple of minutes to flush out the gunk.

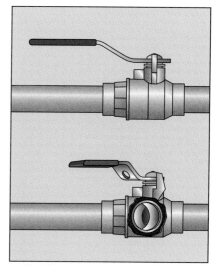

Ball valve
These cost more than the other valves but are more reliable and are easy to shut off quickly. The lever rotates a ball-like gate pierced by an opening. The gate pivots to control the flow of water.

PREVENTING FREEZE-UPS

Ice-cold tap water may taste refreshing, but it also can be a chilling sign that your plumbing is in trouble. Burst pipes from freezing are difficult and expensive to fix, so take precautions if there is reason to believe that your system will not survive the coldest days of the year. New homes with pipes placed near an exterior wall can be as prone to having frozen pipes as poorly insulated older homes. Often the best solution is insulating the wall or ceiling that contains the pipes. This helps keep your home warm and protects your pipes. This page shows some additional ways to prevent plumbing freeze-ups.

YOU'LL NEED...

TIME: About three hours to prepare the average home.
SKILLS: Beginner carpentry and plumbing skills.
TOOLS: Knife, flashlight.

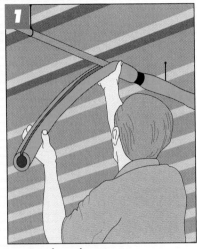

1. Insulate the pipes.
Insulation goes a long way toward preventing freeze-ups, as long as every square inch of pipe—including connections—is protected. Pipe jacketing comes in standard lengths that can be cut with a knife and secured with electrical tape. Ordinary insulation, cut in strips and

bundled around pipes, works equally well for less cost but more labor. In an extremely cold wall or floor, pack the entire cavity with insulation. Also consider insulating long hot water runs, especially those that pass through unheated spaces. The added insulation will conserve water-heating energy.

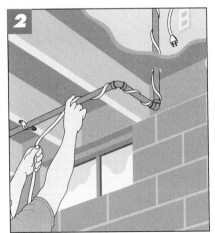

2. Wrap pipes with heat tape.
Electric heat tape draws only modest amounts of current, so it is safe and inexpensive to use. Wrap tape around the pipe, and plug the tape into a receptacle. A thermostat turns the tape on and off as needed. However, tape will not work during a power outage— the very time when the protection may be most needed.

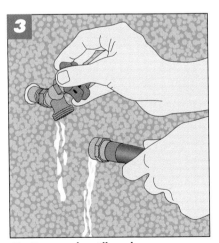

3. Protect the sill cock.
Before winter, remove and drain garden hoses to prevent them from splitting. Shut off the water leading to the sill cock, allow it to drain, and leave it open. If there is no indoor shutoff, install one (see page 30), or install a freeze-proof sill cock—an improvement that may be required by local codes.

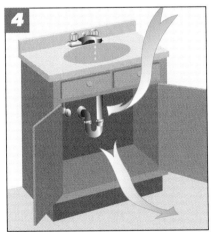

4. Precautions for very cold days
As a preventive measure on extremely cold days, turn on the faucets that have vulnerable parts, and let water trickle constantly. If there is a cabinet underneath, open its doors to let room heat warm the pipes. Use a small lamp to warm pipes that run through cold areas.

WINTERIZING A HOUSE

If you're leaving a house or cabin for an extended period of time during the winter, you don't have to leave the heat on in order to avoid plumbing disasters. You can save money by turning off your utilities and winterizing, which involves shutting off the water supply and draining the whole plumbing system. If you have a private water system, the process is slightly more involved—you'll also have to drain the holding tank and any water-treating apparatus. The result will be peace of mind that the plumbing system is safely dormant, without the expense of keeping the home fires burning.

YOU'LL NEED...

TIME: About four hours to winterize a modest house.
SKILLS: Disconnecting pipes.
TOOLS: Pipe wrench, Crescent wrench, bucket.

1. Drain the system.
Have the water department shut off the water valve outside your home, or do it yourself. Then open every faucet in the house, starting at the top of the system. Shut down and drain the water heater (see page 58). Detach drain hoses on dish and clothes washers.

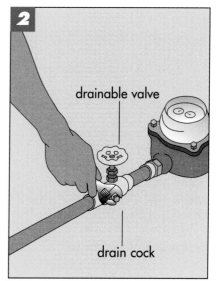

2. Open valves and unions.
Look to see if you have a drainable valve or two—often they are near the water meter. Open the drain cock on each. Drain supply lines completely. If you find a low-lying pipe that doesn't have a faucet or drain cock, open a union where two pipes join (see pages 24–25).

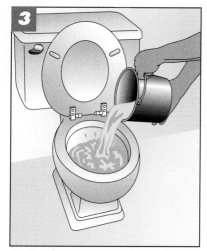

3. Replace water with antifreeze.
Flush toilets, then pour a gallon of antifreeze solution (automotive antifreeze mixed with water, according to directions on the container) into the bowl. This will start a mild flushing action. Some of it will

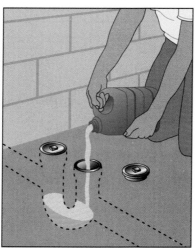

remain in the toilet's trap. Pour antifreeze solution into all fixtures with a trap—sinks, showers, bathtubs, and the washing-machine standpipe. If your house has a main house trap, fill the elbow portion with full-strength antifreeze.

HOME AGAIN

After returning to your winterized house, follow these steps, in order:

- Turn all faucets off, including the sill cock. Remove any aerators on the faucets, and clean if necessary.
- Reconnect all disconnected pipes, and close down all drainable valves.
- Turn on the main water-supply valve.
- Turn all the faucets on slowly, beginning at the sill cock. The water will "spit" out for a while, then assume a normal flow.
- Replace the aerators.

FIXING LEAKS AND FROZEN PIPES

Water escaping from a pipe can wreak havoc in your house. Even a tiny leak that is left to drip day and night will soon rot away everything in its vicinity. A pipe that freezes and bursts can produce a major flood.

As soon as you spot a leak, shut off the water to take pressure off the line. Then locate exactly where the problem is. If the pipe is not visible, this may be difficult, because water can run quite a ways along the outside of the pipe, a floor joist, or a subfloor. Eventually, any leaking pipe must be replaced (see pages 12–27). Here are emergency measures to temporarily stop the flow.

YOU'LL NEED...
TIME: An hour or so to clamp or apply epoxy to a leak.
SKILLS: No special skills needed.
TOOLS: Screwdriver, putty knife.

Wrap with tape.
For a pinhole leak, dry off the pipe, and wrap it tightly with several layers of electrician's tape. Wrap it about 6 inches on either side of the hole. This is extremely temporary, but the tape should hold while you make a trip to the hardware store for a pipe clamp and rubber gasket.

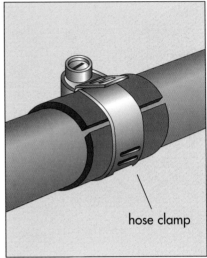

hose clamp

Apply a clamp.
An automotive hose clamp with a piece of rubber—both available at any hardware store—makes a somewhat better leak-stopper. Again, it works only for pinhole leaks. Wrap the rubber around the pipe, and tighten up the clamp. Be sure that the clamp itself is placed directly over the hole.

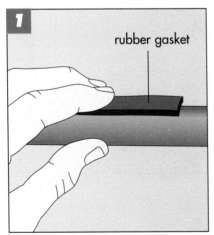

rubber gasket

1. To install a pipe clamp, position the gasket.
The best temporary solution to a leaking pipe is a pipe clamp specially made for this purpose. It will seal small gashes, cracks, and pinhole leaks. It also is semipermanent—expect it to last several years. Position the rubber gasket so the hole is centered under it.

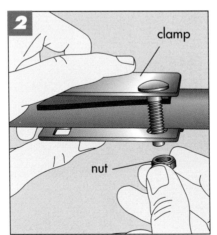

clamp

nut

2. Tighten the clamp.
Assemble the clamp pieces around the gasket, and tighten. Take care that the gasket does not move as you work. Tighten all four nuts evenly, working from nut to nut until all are tight.

EXPERTS' INSIGHT

IT MAY NOT BE A LEAK...
If a pipe shows drips all along its length, it may be condensing water from humid air rather than leaking. Wrap it with insulation to stop the condensation (see page 32).

OR IT MAY BE MORE
An isolated leak may be a sign that pipes are aging. The galvanized pipe common to older homes tends to rust from the inside out. Once a leak appears, expect others to follow. If the pipes in your house have begun to deteriorate, buy a supply of pipe clamps to fit your lines.

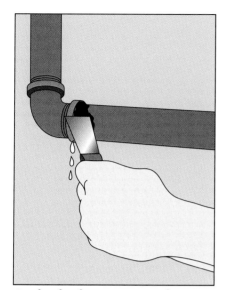

Apply plumber's epoxy at fittings.

If the leak is coming from a fitting, don't try to clamp it. Your best bet is plumber's epoxy. Unless the leak is a real gusher, don't shut off the water. The epoxy comes in two parts. Cut a piece of each, and knead them together until the color is uniform. Pack the epoxy into the connection by pushing it in with your thumb or a putty knife. Pack it until the leak stops.

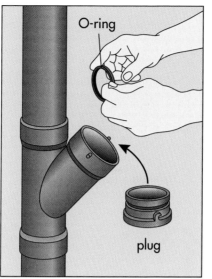

Seal a leaking clean-out.

Drain lines are less leak-prone than supply lines. Once in a while, however, a clean-out plug may seep waste water. Warn everyone in the household not to use any fixtures. Remove the plug (it may screw out or pull out). Reseal screw-in plugs by applying Teflon tape to the male threads. If it has an O-ring, replace it.

Tighten joints in cast-iron pipe.

If you have a leak at the joint of cast-iron pipes, it is usually easy to deal with. For the hub-and-spigot type shown here, use a hammer and chisel to tamp down the soft lead that fills the joint. Don't whack the pipe hard—you could crack it. If you have the no-hub system (see page 87), tightening the clamp will likely stop the leak.

To thaw exposed frozen pipes, heat with a blow dryer ...

Open the faucet the pipe supplies so any steam can escape. If it is exposed, apply heat directly with a hair dryer or a heat gun (turned to its lowest setting). Move the dryer or gun back and forth—don't hold it in one spot.

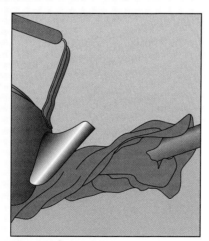

or pour hot water.

Another solution for an exposed frozen pipe is to wrap a cloth around it, then pour boiling water over the cloth. Allow the water to cool, pour again, and repeat until the pipe is thawed. Be sure a faucet is open while you do this so steam can escape.

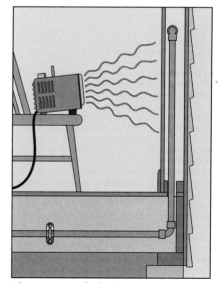

Thaw concealed pipes.

If the pipes are concealed, thawing will take more time. Open a faucet. Beam a heat lamp or electric space heater at the wall containing the pipe. Monitor closely to make sure the heat doesn't damage the wall surface.

IDENTIFYING STEM FAUCETS

When a faucet develops a leak—most often, a drip from the spout or a leak around the base—the problem is usually easy to fix. Very likely, you'll be able to purchase a repair kit for your type of faucet. Repair techniques vary from faucet to faucet, but in most cases you can easily do it yourself. When buying replacement parts, take the old unit to the store. If the faucet cannot be repaired, it is not difficult to replace it with a new one (see pages 50–51).

The first step is to identify the type of faucet you have. The anatomy drawings here and on pages 40, 42, 44, and 46 show you the various types.

The most common type is the seat-and-washer faucet, often called a compression faucet. All stem faucets have separate hot and cold controls. In its off position, the stem compresses a flexible washer on the stem into a beveled seat located in the faucet base, stopping the flow of water. As the washer wears, you have to apply more and more pressure to turn off the unit. That's when dripping usually begins.

Two newer versions are types of washerless stem faucets—cartridge and diaphragm. The cartridge type rotates rather than raising and lowering to control flow. It uses a rubber seal and O-rings. The diaphragm type uses a durable diaphragm instead of the flexible washer.

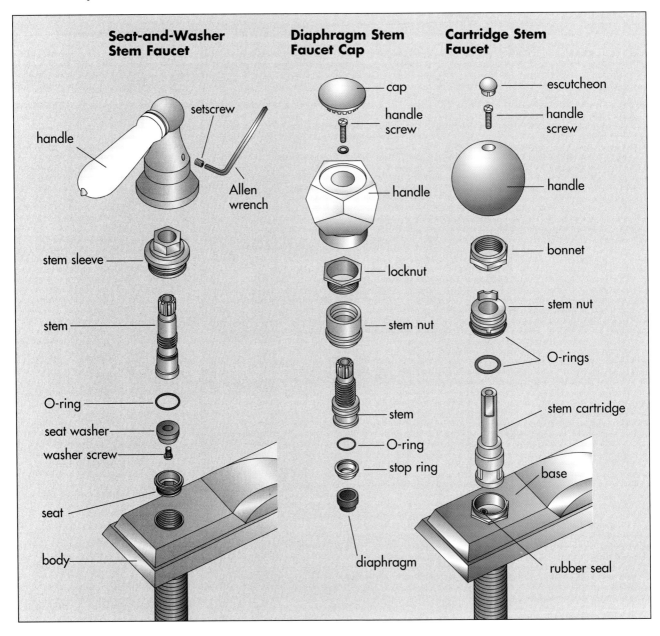

Seat-and-Washer Stem Faucet — handle, setscrew, Allen wrench, stem sleeve, stem, O-ring, seat washer, washer screw, seat, body

Diaphragm Stem Faucet Cap — cap, handle screw, handle, locknut, stem nut, stem, O-ring, stop ring, diaphragm

Cartridge Stem Faucet — escutcheon, handle screw, handle, bonnet, stem nut, O-rings, stem cartridge, base, rubber seal

PULLING OUT HANDLES AND STEMS

The first step in replacing the inner workings of a stem faucet is to pull out the handles and stems and take them to the store when you buy proper replacement parts. If you can identify the faucet by brand name, it will be easier to find the right part. Often no brand name is visible, so you'll have to take out the stem and compare it with the drawings on pages 36, 40, 42, 44, and 46.
Note: *When working on faucets, shut off the water.*

YOU'LL NEED...
TIME: About 15 minutes, unless the parts are stuck.
SKILLS: No special skills needed.
TOOLS: Screwdriver, tongue-and-groove pliers, possibly a handle puller.

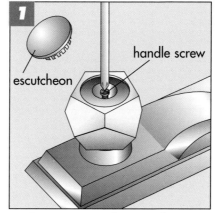

1. Remove escutcheon and screw.
If your handle is round, it is probably connected to the stem with a screw from the top. You may have to pry off an escutcheon (usually marked "H" or "C") to get to it. Some handles are attached with setscrews—see the handle on the seat-and-washer stem faucet on page 36. Remove the setscrew with an Allen wrench, and pull the handle off.

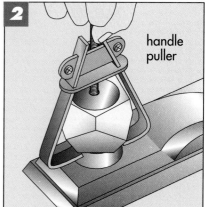

2. Pull out handle and stem.
Usually, the handle will come out if you pull it up firmly or pry it up with a screwdriver. Take care not to mar the finish on the handle. If it is really stuck, use a handle puller that grips the handle from underneath and draws the handle off the stem. Once the handle is off, unscrew the stem with pliers.

REPLACING SEAT WASHERS

Perhaps the most common plumbing repair of all is replacing a seat washer. If yours is a seat-and-washer stem faucet, the washer often becomes worn. Most commonly, there is a depression running in a ring around the washer, or the washer has begun to crumble with old age.

If a washer wears out quickly, the seat is damaged and nicks the washer every time you shut the water off, making the faucet drip (see page 39 to replace a seat).

YOU'LL NEED...
TIME: About 30 minutes, plus a trip to your supplier if you don't have the right washer.
SKILLS: No special skills needed.
TOOLS: Screwdriver.

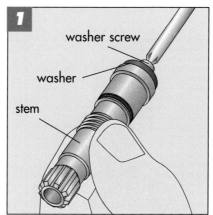

1. Remove the old washer.
Examine your washer. If it is damaged in any way, remove the washer screw, and pull the old washer off. Clean away any debris or deposits from the bottom of the stem. Take your stem and old washer to your supplier if you are not sure how to select a new washer that will fit.

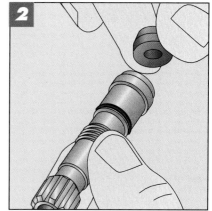

2. Insert a new washer.
Find a washer the exact same size and shape as the old one. If the old washer has been squashed out of shape, this may be difficult to determine, so double-check by slipping the new washer onto the bottom of the stem. It should fit fairly snugly. Replace and tighten the screw, and reinstall the stem.

REPAIRING DIAPHRAGM AND CARTRIDGE STEMS

Diaphragm and cartridge stem faucets are just as easy to repair as seat-and-washer stem faucets. Often the most difficult part of the job is finding the right parts. There are hundreds of O-ring sizes. The safest way is to remove the stem, take it to your supplier, and show it to a salesperson. That way, the O-rings fit the stem exactly.
NOTE: *Be sure to shut off the water before removing stems.*

YOU'LL NEED...

TIME: Just a few minutes, once you've got the right parts, the faucet handle is removed, and the stem unscrewed.
SKILLS: No special skills needed.
TOOLS: Small screwdriver or a sharp-pointed tool.

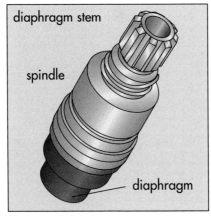

Replace a diaphragm.
Sometimes called a top hat stem, a diaphragm stem has a diaphragm that functions much like a seat washer. To replace it, simply pull off the worn diaphragm, and snap a new one on.

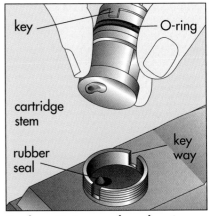

Replace O-ring, seal, and spring.
For a cartridge stem, fix leaks by replacing the seal and O-rings. Remove the rubber seal from the base of the faucet with the sharpened end of a pencil; a small spring will come out as well. Remove the O-ring by hand, or carefully pry it off with a sharp tool. Lubricate the new parts lightly with heatproof grease after you install them.

REPAIRING LEAKS FROM HANDLES

If the faucet leaks around the handle, you'll need to remove the stem to get at the source of the problem. Older faucets have packing wound around the top of the spindle to keep water from seeping out the top. Don't be put off by this old-fashioned material; it is easy to replace, and new packing will last for years. Newer stems have O-rings. Once you have the stem out, inspect the rest of the faucet, and replace any parts that look as if they're starting to wear out. **NOTE:** *Be sure to shut off the water.*

YOU'LL NEED...

TIME: Fifteen minutes to repack a spindle and replace an O-ring.
SKILLS: No special skills needed.
TOOLS: None.

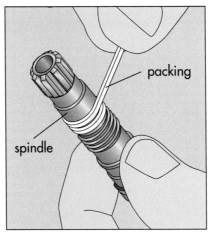

Wrap on new packing string.
If your faucet has packing wound around the spindle just under the packing nut (see page 31), remove all of it and clean the spindle. Choose either Teflon tape or strand packing, and wind it fairly tight. Leave just enough room so the packing nut can be screwed on when the stem is replaced.

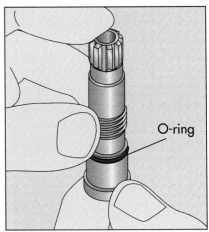

Replace the O-ring.
Newer stems have an O-ring instead of packing. Simply remove the old O-ring, and replace it with one that fits exactly. Lightly lubricate the O-ring with heatproof grease after you install it and before you reinstall the stem.

REPLACING AND GRINDING SEATS

When the spout of a stem faucet (either a seat-and-washer or a diaphragm type) leaks, be sure to inspect the seat as well as the washer or diaphragm. If the seat is pitted or scored, it is scraping the washer or diaphragm every time you turn the faucet off. It will quickly damage a seat washer, and your faucet will leak again even if you've fixed it.

If the seat is damaged, it is best to replace it. Sometimes, however, it is hard to extract the old one. In those cases, try grinding it smooth with a special tool.

YOU'LL NEED...

TIME: About 20 minutes to replace or grind a seat, once you have the part or tool.
SKILLS: No special skills needed, but you must work carefully.
TOOLS: Flashlight, seat wrench or seat cutter.

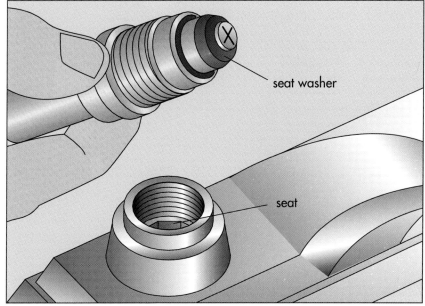

Inspect the seat.
Remove the stem (see page 37), and inspect the washer or diaphragm. If it looks cut up, the likely cause is a damaged seat. Whether the washer or diaphragm looks damaged or not, examine the seat, first by looking at it with a flashlight, then by feeling with your finger. If it appears or feels less than smooth, your washer or diaphragm will have a hard time sealing water off when you crank down on the handle. The seat needs to be replaced or ground smooth with a seat grinder.

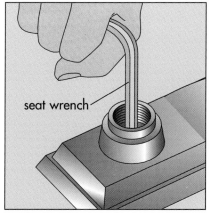

Replace a damaged seat.
Though it is sometimes possible to remove a seat with a screwdriver, this is risky—you may damage the seat so that it cannot be removed. Purchase a seat wrench, which is designed to remove seats of various sizes. Insert it into the seat, push down firmly, and turn counterclockwise. Install the new seat with the same tool.

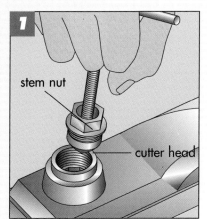

1. Use a seat grinder for a seat that cannot be removed.
Purchase a seat grinder. Slip the stem nut over the shaft of the seat grinder—it helps stabilize the grinder. Select a cutter head that fits easily inside the body and is as wide as the seat.

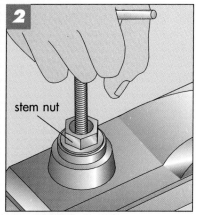

2. Rotate the grinder.
Screw the stem nut into the faucet body to hold the shaft securely without wobbling. Push down gently, and turn the handle clockwise three full rotations. Remove the grinder, and inspect the seat with a flashlight. If it is not smooth, try again.

REPAIRING CARTRIDGE FAUCETS

Most washerless faucets use a combination of seals and O-rings to control and direct water. A cartridge faucet, (manufactured by Kohler, Moen, Price-Pfister, and others) uses a series of strategically placed O-rings and/or seals.

In the type shown, the cartridge O-rings fit snugly against the inside of the faucet body. One O-ring forms a seal between the hot and cold supply lines. The others protect against leaks from the spout and from under the handle. On swivel-spout models, another ring protects against leaks from under the spout. Raising the handle lifts the stem so it slides upward inside the cartridge. Holes in the stem align with the openings in the cartridge in various combinations.

Other types have fewer O-rings and use other types of seals. Repair kits are available for each manufacturer and model.

When this type of faucet leaks, you can replace either the O-rings or the cartridge itself if it has corroded. Because the design is simple, repairs usually don't take long. In fact, disassembly is usually the bulk of the work, and your only problem may be finding the retainer clip that holds the cartridge in the faucet.

YOU'LL NEED...

TIME: About an hour, once you have the replacement parts.
SKILLS: No special skills needed.
TOOLS: Screwdriver, needle-nose and tongue-and-groove pliers.

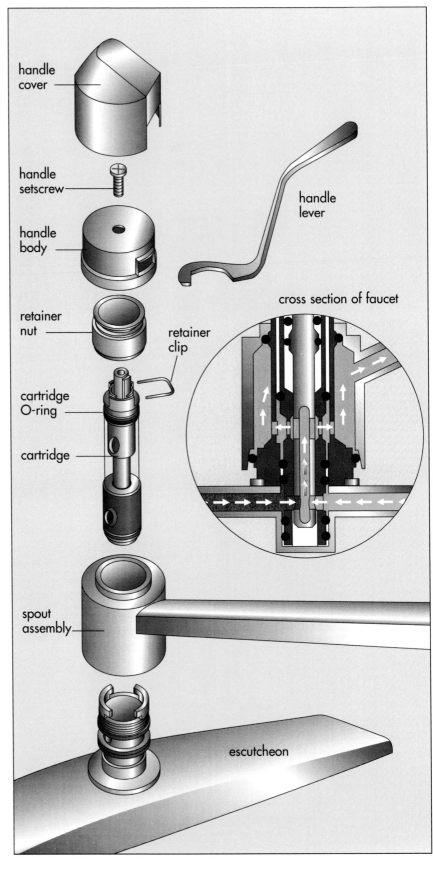

handle cover

handle setscrew

handle body

retainer nut

retainer clip

cartridge O-ring

cartridge

spout assembly

handle lever

cross section of faucet

escutcheon

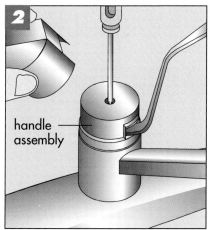

1. Remove the handle housing.
NOTE: *Shut off the water, and drain the line.* Cartridge faucets vary in design from model to model, but you disassemble most of them as follows: Pry off the decorative cover that conceals the handle screw. Be careful not to crack the cover in doing so; most are made of plastic. You may need to remove an external retaining clip to get the cover off.

2. Remove handle assembly.
Cover the drain with a rag to avoid losing any small parts. Beneath the handle housing is a setscrew that holds the handle in place. Remove the handle screw, and lift off the handle body and lever. If there is no retainer nut (next step), lift out the spout.

3. Remove retainer nut and spout.
Swivel-spout models will have a retainer nut. Unscrew it, then lift off the spout.

You'll need to disassemble some models differently. Pry off the cap on top of the faucet, remove the screw, and remove the handle by tilting it back and pulling up. Then remove the plastic threaded retaining ring.

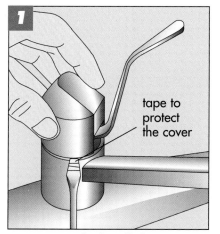

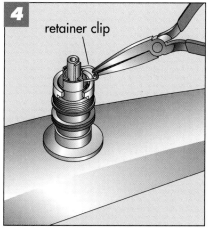

4. Pull out the retainer clip.
Depending on the model you have, you may need to lift off a cylindrical sleeve to get at the cartridge. You should now be able to see the retainer clip, a metal piece that holds the cartridge in place. Use needle-nose pliers to remove the clip from its slot. Be careful not to misplace it.

5. Remove the cartridge.
With tongue-and-groove pliers, lift the cartridge from the faucet body. Take note of the position of the cartridge ears, and be sure that when you put the cartridge back in, its ears are facing in the same direction. Otherwise, hot and cold will be reversed. If you are replacing O-rings, give them a light coating of heatproof lubricant. When reassembling the faucet, tighten firmly, but don't crank down hard—there are lots of plastic parts that can crack.

EXPERTS' INSIGHT

BUY QUALITY REPLACEMENT PARTS

Your local hardware store or building supply center may have replacement parts that are inexpensive but a bit flimsy. As long as you are investing a fair amount of your time in making the repair, pay the relatively small extra cost to install long-lasting parts. It is usually best to buy replacement parts made by the faucet manufacturer, rather than by a general supplier that only makes replacement parts.

If you cannot find the manufacturer's name on the faucet, remove the parts and take them to your supplier to ensure the right match.

REPAIRING ROTATING BALL FAUCETS

Inside a rotating ball faucet a slotted ball sits atop a pair of spring-loaded seals. When the handle is lowered to the "off" position, this ball, held tight against the seals by the faucet's cap, closes off the water supply. This type of faucet is often called a Delta faucet, after the primary manufacturer of this faucet type, the Delta Faucet Co.

As the handle is raised, the ball rotates in such a way that the openings align with the supply line ports. This allows water to pass through the ball and out the spout. Moving the handle to the left allows more hot water to flow out; moving it to the right adds cold water.

Most leaks can be fixed by replacing the ball and gaskets in the faucet (see page 43). In addition, seals and springs can give out and need replacement.

These faucets also can spring leaks from around the handle and, with swivel-spout models, from under the base of the spout. Handle leaks indicate that the adjusting ring has loosened or the seal above the ball is worn.

Leaks from under the spout result from O-ring failure. Inspect the rings encircling the body and, on units with diverter valves for a sprayer, the valve O-ring. Replace the O-rings if they look worn.

CAUTION!
To avoid damage to flooring and walls, turn off supply lines or the main water valve.

YOU'LL NEED...
TIME: About two hours to rebuild and reassemble a faucet.
SKILLS: Patience, an eye for detail.
TOOLS: Adjustable pliers, wrench that comes with the rebuild kit, awl or other sharp-pointed tool.

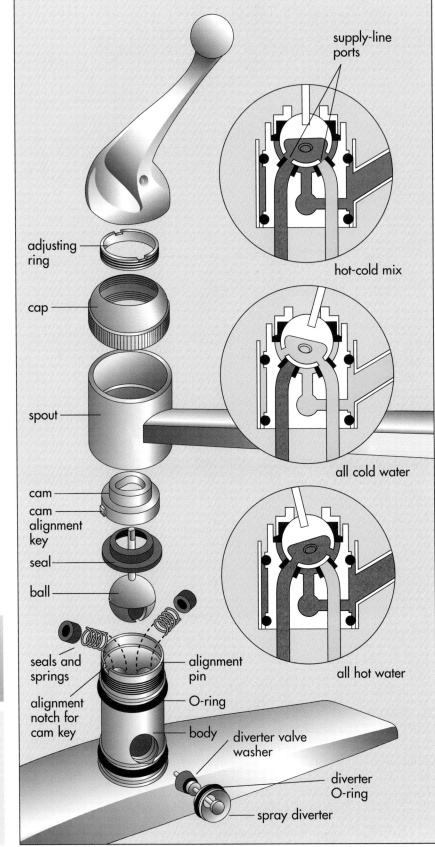

supply-line ports

hot-cold mix

all cold water

all hot water

adjusting ring

cap

spout

cam

cam alignment key

seal

ball

seals and springs

alignment notch for cam key

alignment pin

O-ring

body

diverter valve washer

diverter O-ring

spray diverter

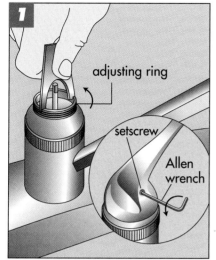

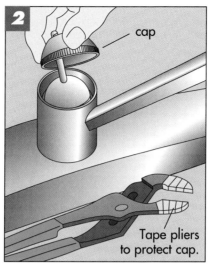

1. Remove handle and cap.
Shut off the water supply, and drain the lines by lifting straight up on the handle. Using an Allen wrench, loosen the setscrew that holds the handle in place (see inset above). Loosen the adjusting ring using the wrench that comes packed with your purchased repair kit.

2. Disassemble cam, ball, spout.
Unscrew the cap with cloth- or tape-covered adjustable pliers. Lift out the cam assembly, the ball, and, in the case of a swivel-spout faucet, the spout. The spout fits tightly against the O-rings of the body, so it may prove stubborn. Be careful not to scratch the spout as you remove it.

3. Remove seals and springs.
To remove worn seals and springs from the body, insert a pencil into each seal to pull them out. Check for blockage at the supply inlet ports, scrape away any buildup, then insert new springs and seals.

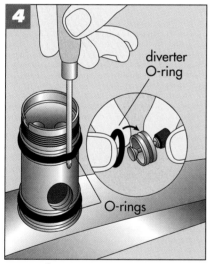

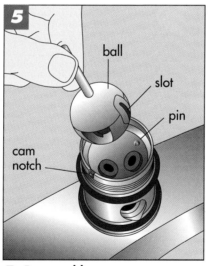

4. Replace O-rings.
If the faucet has a swivel spout, pry the O-rings away from the body using an awl or other sharp-pointed tool. Roll the new ones down over the body until they rest in the appropriate grooves. Replace the diverter O-ring in the same way. Lightly coat the O-rings and the inside of the spout with heatproof grease.

5. Reassemble.
Be sure to align the slot in the side of the ball with the pin inside the body. Also, the key on the cam assembly fits into a corresponding notch in the body. Hand-tighten the cap, and tighten the adjusting ring for a good seal between the ball and the cam. If it leaks, tighten further.

EXPERTS' INSIGHT

Select quality parts
Repair kits of lesser or greater quality are available for this type of faucet. Some include plastic balls; others include longer-lasting metal parts. If your hardware store only has the cheaper kit, try a plumbing supply store for a kit with longer-lasting, though more expensive, parts.

Consider a complete rebuild
When a faucet is old enough to have one part wear out, other parts will soon wear out as well. As long as you are fixing one part of the faucet, do a complete rebuild.

REPAIRING CERAMIC DISK FAUCETS

When you raise the faucet lever of a disk faucet, the upper disk in the cartridge slides across the lower disk, allowing water to enter the mixing chamber. The higher you raise the lever, the more water enters through the inlet ports of the faucet body. Moving the lever from side to side determines whether hot or cold water or a mixture of the two comes out of the spout.

The disk assembly itself, generally made of a long-lasting ceramic material, rarely needs replacing. However, the inlet ports can become clogged with mineral deposits. If this happens, simply disassemble the faucet, and scrape away the crusty buildup.

If the faucet leaks at the base of the lever, one or more of the inlet seals on the cartridge may need replacing. See page 45 for how to replace the seals and the cartridge. While the faucet is dismantled, replace all of the seals. If one is worn, the others don't have long to live. Before you go to your supplier, get the brand name of your faucet from the faucet body—or take the disk assembly along. You probably can buy a repair kit with the parts you need.

YOU'LL NEED...

TIME: About an hour for repairs.
SKILLS: No special skills needed.
TOOLS: Small screwdriver, tongue-and-groove pliers.

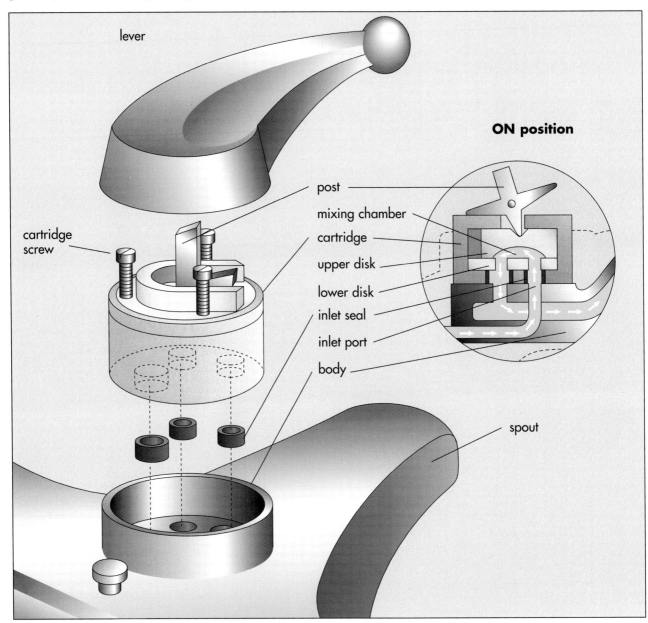

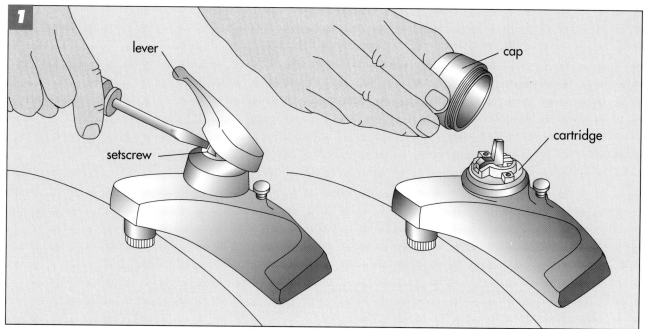

1. Remove the lever and cap.
Note: *Shut off the water.*
Under the lever you'll see a setscrew that holds the lever to the lever post. Use an appropriately sized screwdriver to unscrew the setscrew—don't try to unscrew it with a knife or you may damage it. Loosen the screw until you can raise the lever off the post. You may have to gently pry it off with a large screwdriver.

Lift off or unscrew the decorative cap that covers the cartridge. Then loosen the screws holding the cartridge to the faucet body, and lift out the cartridge.

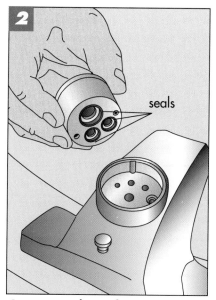

2. Remove the seals.
On the underside of the cartridge you'll find a set of seals. Pull them out with your fingers, or carefully use a sharp-pointed tool, being careful not to scratch the cartridge.

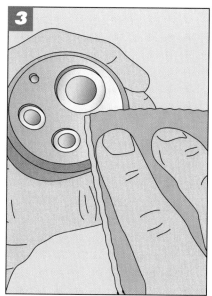

3. Clean the openings.
Check the openings for sediment buildup, and clean it away. Use a nonmetallic scrubber or a sponge.

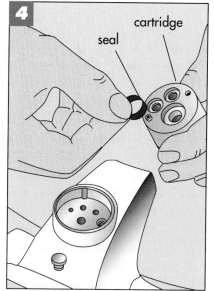

4. Replace the seals, reassemble.
Put the seals back, or install replacement seals. Reassemble the faucet. Turn the water back on, and test. If the faucet continues to leak after you have cleaned the cartridge and replaced the seals, install a new cartridge.

REPAIRING GASKETED CARTRIDGE FAUCETS

Gasketed cartridge faucets use a gasket with a group of openings at the bottom of the faucet cartridge to mix hot and cold water and direct water to the spout. Newer models have ceramic cartridges; older ones have plastic.

YOU'LL NEED...

TIME: About an hour, plus shopping time.
SKILLS: Basic plumbing skills.
TOOLS: Screwdriver, tongue-and-groove pliers.

Note: *Shut off the water before disassembling.*

If you're trying to fix a leak from the body of the faucet, first try tightening the cap by hand—do not crank down on it with a wrench. If that doesn't work, disassemble the faucet, and replace the two O-rings. Coat them lightly with heatproof grease.

To disassemble, pry off the escutcheon, and remove the lever screw. Lift off the lever, and unscrew the cap and the retainer nut. The other parts will pull out.

If you're trying to fix a drip from the spout, the cartridge probably needs to be replaced. Check the retainer nut as well. If its threads are stripped, replace it.

These parts are specific to the faucet manufacturer, so take the old parts with you when you go to the store to make sure you buy the right replacement parts.

If the faucet operates stiffly, debris may have built up in the cartridge. In most cases, it will be more trouble to clean than it is to buy a new cartridge—just replace the cartridge.

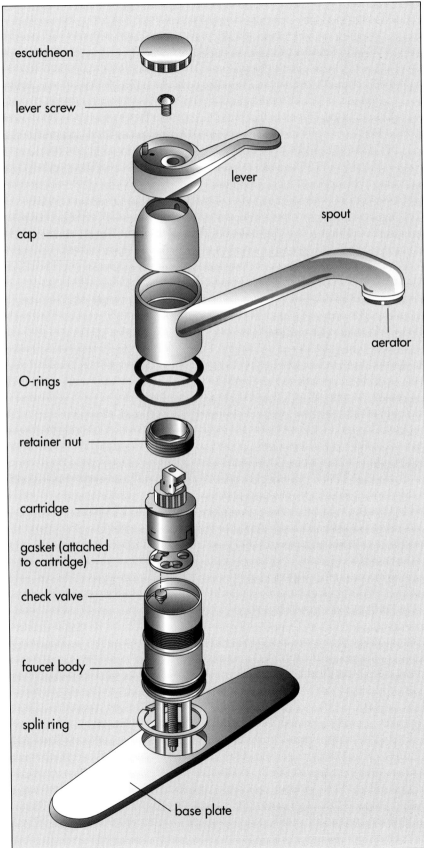

escutcheon

lever screw

lever

spout

cap

O-rings

aerator

retainer nut

cartridge

gasket (attached to cartridge)

check valve

faucet body

split ring

base plate

SEALING LEAKY BASE PLATES

If you find water in the cabinet below the sink, it could be from three places—the supply lines, the drain, or water leaking into the cabinet from under the faucet base plate. The problem may be solved by simply tightening the supply lines (see page 49). If the leak comes from the drain, see page 72. If neither of those is the cause, you may have a leaky base plate that allows splashed water to seep through mounting holes. Follow the steps on this page to solve this last problem.

YOU'LL NEED...
TIME: Two hours to remove, seal, and replace the faucet.
SKILLS: Basic plumbing skills.
TOOLS: Putty knife, tongue-and-groove pliers or basin wrench.

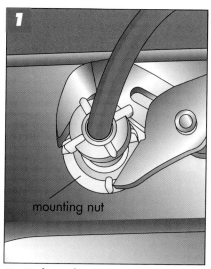
mounting nut

1. Tighten the mounting nuts.
It may be that your faucet is not held tight against the sink. Get under your sink in as comfortable a position as possible, and tighten the mounting nuts. If you can't turn them with pliers, use a basin wrench (see page 50). If this does not solve the problem, try Step 2.

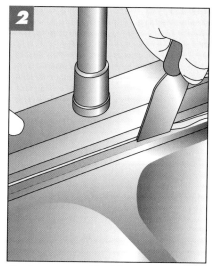

2. Loosen, stuff with putty.
First try to fix the leak without removing the faucet. Loosen the mounting nuts enough to raise the faucet base about a half inch above the sink. Scrape out any hardened gunk. Holding the base plate just above the sink, stuff plumber's putty under it evenly. Retighten the mounting nuts. If it continues to leak, proceed to Step 3.

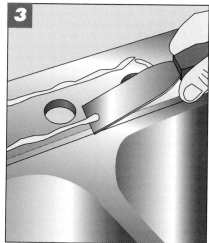

3. Remove the faucet and scrape.
NOTE: *Shut off the water, and drain the line.* To entirely reseat the base plate, remove the faucet. Disconnect the supply lines, remove the mounting nuts, and pull the faucet out. Scrape any old putty away, and clean the area thoroughly. Take care not to scratch the sink.

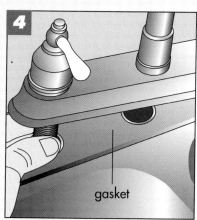
gasket

4. Replace the gasket ...
If the faucet has a gasket, throw it out, and replace it with a new one. If you have trouble finding a replacement, a new gasket can be made by purchasing a piece of rubber of a similar thickness. You can use the old gasket as a pattern, and cut out a new one.

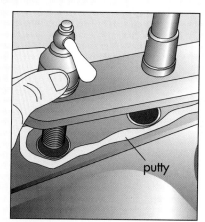
putty

or apply new putty.
Many plumbers believe putty lasts longer than gaskets, so even if your faucet has a gasket, you may want to discard it and apply putty instead. Roll a rope of putty, about $1/4$ inch in diameter, and apply it to the sink or to the underside of the faucet. Reinstall the faucet, and check for leaks.

FIXING SPRAYERS, DIVERTERS, AND AERATORS

Sink sprayers can be obstructed at the connections, gaskets, and the nozzle. If water doesn't come out of the sprayer, the problem is most likely a faulty diverter valve: You can replace either the rubber seal or the diverter. Remove the diverter and take it to your supplier to be sure you get the correct replacement.

Diverters vary in shape and location, but all work in much the same way. When water isn't flowing toward the spray outlet, the valve remains open and directs the water flow toward the spout. When you press the sprayer lever, the flow of water shifts toward the sprayer head.

If your faucet has low water pressure, check the aerator. Aerators may develop leaks if their seals are worn, or they can get clogged up.

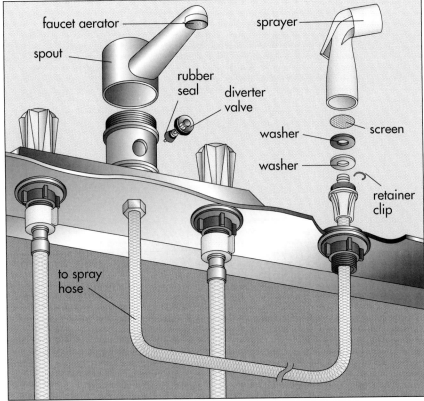

YOU'LL NEED...

TIME: One to two hours.
SKILLS: Basic plumbing skills and attention to detail.
TOOLS: Tongue-and-groove pliers, old toothbrush, awl, or nail.

From diverter to sprayer
To find the diverter in a typical one-handle faucet, remove the spout; it's usually located in front.

If you get low or no water pressure from the sprayer, first check the hose for kinks. A slow stream of water coupled with some water coming from the spout may signal a stuck valve or a worn washer or O-ring. Replace the rubber parts or the diverter valve. Or, the sprayer screen may be clogged (see below).

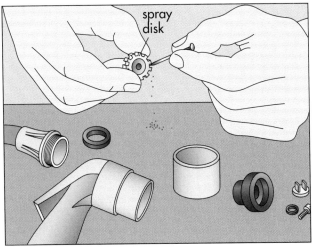

Troubleshoot the sprayer.
Minerals may be restricting the flow of water through the sprayer. Clean the spray disk with an awl or a nail as shown. Replace any worn parts, and tighten all the connections.

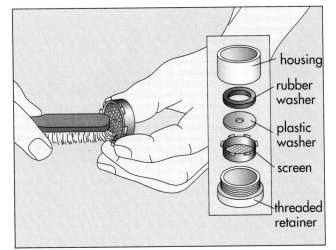

Clean the aerator.
To clean out the aerator, unscrew it from the faucet spout and disassemble it, brush all the parts clean, and soak the pieces in vinegar overnight. If it is heavily clogged, just buy a new one.

STOPPING LEAKS IN FLEXIBLE SUPPLY LINES

*T*here are three basic types of flexible supply lines. Plain or chrome-plated copper tubing uses ferrules and nuts for connections. Flexible plastic lines use knobby ends that take the place of ferrules. Flexible supply lines—either plastic or stainless-steel-braided—use nuts preattached at each end. The last type is the easiest to use. Just make sure you buy lines that are long enough.

YOU'LL NEED...

TIME: An hour for most repairs and replacements.
SKILLS: Tightening and loosening nuts in tight places.
TOOLS: Basin wrench or tongue-and-groove pliers, adjustable wrenches.

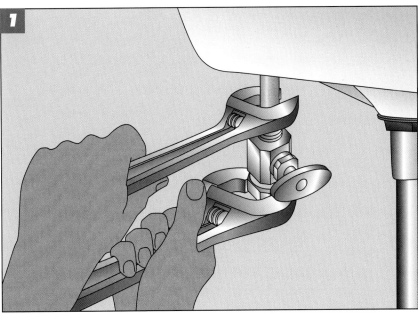

1. Tighten the nuts.
Often, the solution is simple—just tighten the nut at the point where you see a leak. However, take care not to crank down too hard. You can crack the nut or strip the threads. Use only adjustable wrenches, not pipe wrenches. If the leak persists, loosen the nuts, and recoat the threads or ferrules with Teflon tape or pipe joint compound as shown in Step 2.

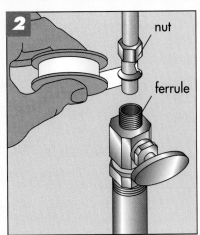

2. Coat the ferrule ...
Note: *Be sure to shut off the water, and drain the line.*
If you have a tubing-and-ferrule arrangement, remove the nut, and pull the line at least partway out. Take care not to kink it. Coat the ferrule with joint compound, or wrap it with Teflon tape. Hook it back up, tighten, and test.

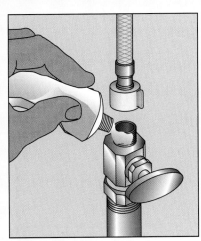

or the threads.
If you have a plastic or braided flexible line, shut off the water, unscrew the nut, and apply joint compound or Teflon tape to the male threads of the shutoff valve or the faucet. Reconnect, tighten, and test.

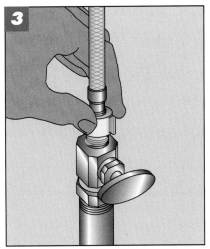

3. Install a new line.
If these measures do not solve your problem quickly, don't keep fussing with the old line. Shut off the water, and remove the old supply line. Buy a new flexible line, apply Teflon tape or joint compound to the male threads, and screw the new flexible line on. Tighten both ends, and test.

REPLACING FAUCETS

Even though thousands of styles of faucets have been made and continue to be made, there are few variations in basic design. Bathroom faucets have pop-up drain assemblies, and kitchen faucets may have sprayers.

Also, there are two possibilities for supply connections: Your faucet may have flexible copper supply inlets in the center of the unit, as shown at right, or its inlets may be located under the hot and cold handles, as seen in Step 2 on page 51.

YOU'LL NEED...

TIME: Several hours to remove an old faucet and install a new one.
SKILLS: No special skills needed, but it may be hard work getting the old faucet out.
TOOLS: Tongue-and-groove pliers, basin wrench, screwdriver.

EXPERTS' INSIGHT

MAKING IT EASY

■ The hardest part of the job will be getting at the faucet from underneath. Remove any cabinet doors that may be in the way, hook up a work light, and make your work area as comfortable as possible.

■ If you are installing a sink at the same time as the faucet, attach the faucet to the sink before you install the sink.

■ Often, even penetrating oil won't loosen old locknuts. You may have to knock the nut loose with a hammer and screwdriver.

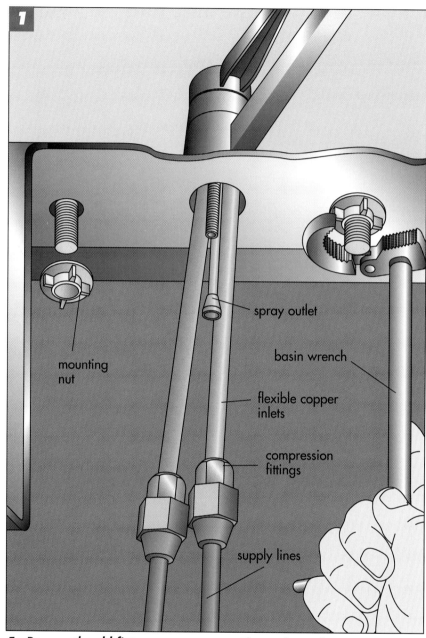

mounting nut

spray outlet

basin wrench

flexible copper inlets

compression fittings

supply lines

1. Remove the old fixture.
Note: *Shut off the water.*
(This illustration shows a faucet with flexible copper inlets.) Before you worm your way into the space below the sink, gather the tools you'll need, as well as some penetrating oil in case the mounting nuts are stuck. It helps to have someone around who can hand you tools as you work.

If your faucet has a sprayer, remove the nuts securing the hose to the faucet body and the spray head to the sink. Unhook the supply lines, and move them out of the way. Use the basin wrench to loosen and remove the mounting nuts holding the faucet body to the sink.

Lift the faucet out from above. Scrape the sink top clean of old putty and mineral deposits.

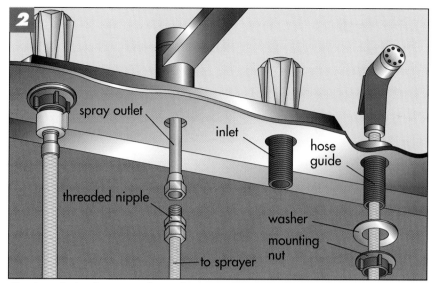

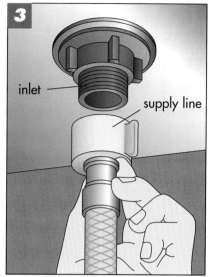

2. Attach the faucet to the sink.

(Here we show a faucet with inlets located under the handles.) Install a gasket or a rope of plumber's putty to the faucet or to the sink (see page 47). Set the faucet in place, making sure it is parallel to the backsplash. Crawl under the sink, and have a helper hold the faucet in position while you work. Screw a washer and mounting nut onto each inlet, and tighten with a basin wrench.

For faucets with sprayers, secure the hose guide to the sink with a washer and mounting nut. Thread the spray hose down through the hole in the guide. Apply pipe joint compound or Teflon tape to the threaded nipple at the end of the hose, and secure it to the spray outlet of the faucet.

3. Connect the supply lines.

Brush the inlet threads with pipe joint compound, or wrap them with Teflon tape. Twist the supply line nut onto the inlet, and tighten first by hand, then with a basin wrench. Connect the other end of the supply line to the shutoff valve in the same way.

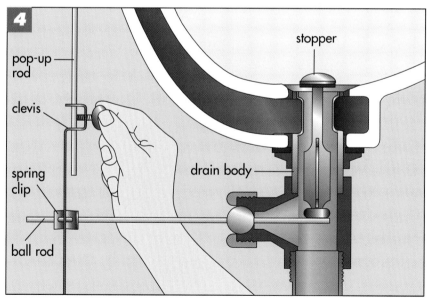

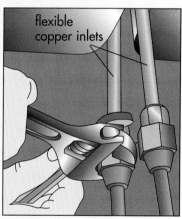

4. Connect and adjust the pop-up drain assembly.

For a bathroom faucet, insert the ball rod into the opening in the drain body, and secure it with the nut provided. Slip the rod through the clevis strap, and secure it with the spring clip. Lower the pop-up rod down through the hole near the rear of the faucet spout and through the holes at the upper end of the clevis strap. Lightly tighten the thumbscrew, and adjust the rod so the stopper seals when the rod is pulled up. When the stopper opens and closes easily, tighten the thumbscrew further to secure the rod.

Connecting to flexible inlets
Some faucets use flexible copper inlets for the water supply. Connect supply lines to these lines in the same way as you would regular inlets, but take special care not to twist the copper tubes. If they become kinked, the faucet will be ruined. Use two wrenches, as shown.

REPAIRING TOILETS

Because it gets used so often, your toilet has a good chance of eventually needing repair. Although some people find the prospect of working on a toilet distasteful, as long as you flush it once or twice before beginning, you will be dealing with clean water only. (If it won't flush, see page 76.) You may find some rust and sediment in the tank.

The inner parts of a toilet are fairly simple. When someone flips the flush handle, a chain reaction of events starts. The handle lifts the trip lever, which in turn pulls a chain that lifts the tank flapper off the flush valve. (In older units, a lift rod raises a tank ball.) As water rushes down through the opening into the bowl, the reservoir of water and the waste in the bowl yield to gravity and pass through the toilet's trap, down through the closet bend, and out a drain line.

Inside the tank, the float (or in older systems the float ball) descends along with the outrushing water until, at a predetermined level, the shutoff rod it attaches to trips the ballcock, which is a water supply valve. At the same time, the tank flapper settles back into the flush valve, stopping water from leaving the tank. The ballcock opens to shoot a new supply of water into the tank through a refill tube and into the bowl through the overflow tube. When the float rises to its filled position, the ballcock shuts the water off.

A wax ring seals the toilet bowl to a flange on the closet bend and keeps water from leaking out onto the floor. A spud gasket seals the tank to the bowl.

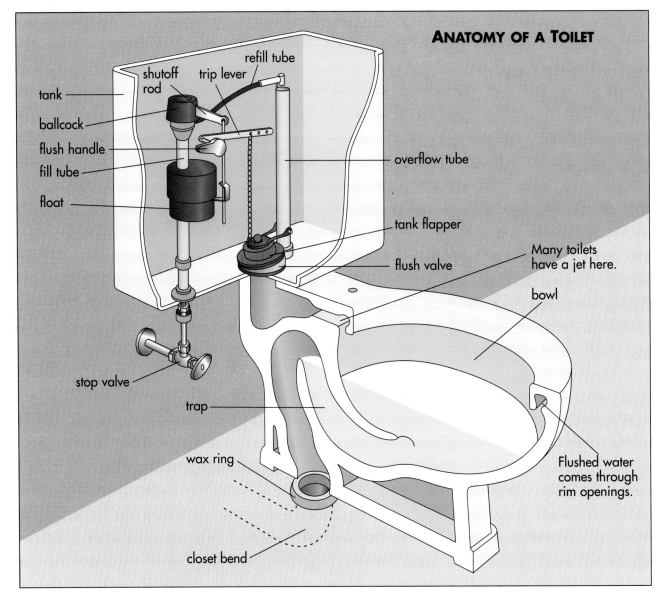

ANATOMY OF A TOILET

tank · shutoff rod · trip lever · refill tube · ballcock · flush handle · fill tube · float · overflow tube · tank flapper · flush valve · Many toilets have a jet here. · bowl · stop valve · trap · Flushed water comes through rim openings. · wax ring · closet bend

TOILET REPAIR CHART

Symptom	Cause	Repair
Water continuously trickles or runs into tank and/or bowl (tank run-on).	Water level is too high.	Adjust trip lever chain, adjust water level in tank, or replace leaky float (see below).
	Flapper or tank ball isn't sealing properly.	Clean the flush valve under the flapper, or replace worn flapper.
	Ballcock is faulty.	Repair or replace ballcock.
Bowl overflows when flushed. Toilet flushes incompletely.	Trap or drain is partially clogged.	Run a toilet auger through the toilet (see page 76), or clear drain (see page 77).
	Trap or bowl is clogged.	
Tank leaks.	Water is spraying up against the lid.	Anchor the refill tube so it sprays into the overflow tube.
	Gasket between tank and bowl is faulty.	Replace the spud gasket.
	Tank is cracked.	Replace the tank.
Bowl leaks. Leak appears as a wet spot on the floor.	Wax ring is not sealing.	Pull up the toilet and replace the wax ring (see page 56).
	Bowl is cracked.	Replace the bowl.
Tank "sweats"—drops of water appear on the outside.	Condensation occurs due to difference in temperature between air and tank water.	Buy an insulation kit and install in the inside of the tank.

FIXING TANK RUN-ON

Most of a toilet's mechanical action goes on inside the flush tank, and that's where most common toilet problems develop. If water continually trickles or flows into the tank and/or bowl, start with the simplest diagnosis: The float may be rising too high, causing water to trickle down the overflow tube. If fixing that doesn't solve the problem, see if the chain is tangled or has fallen off. Check flapper and ballcock (see page 52).

YOU'LL NEED...

TIME: Five minutes to adjust the float; a half hour to adjust and clean the flush valve; one hour to replace a ballcock.
SKILLS: General mechanical aptitude.
TOOLS: Screwdriver, tongue-and-groove pliers.

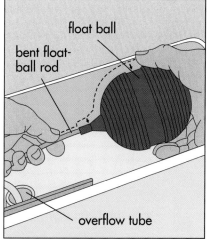

Adjust the float ball.
Remove the tank lid, and look to see if the water level is too high— it should not be passing into the overflow tube. If it is, the water will shut off when you pull up on the float ball. Bend the rod slightly downward so the float ball sits a bit lower. With a float like the one shown on page 52, adjust the clip.

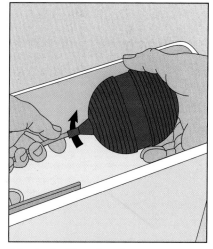

Check the float for damage.
A cracked float takes on water. When this happens, the ball won't rise enough to trip the ballcock. To check out this possibility, agitate the ball. A faulty ball will make a swishing sound. Unscrew a faulty float ball, and replace it with a new one.

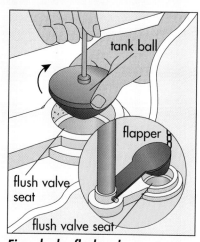

Fix a leaky flush valve seat.
If water continually trickles into the bowl, and perhaps even causes the toilet to weakly flush occasionally, the problem is probably in the flush valve. It has two parts: a flapper or a tank ball, and the flush valve seat into which the flapper or ball drops to seal the bottom of the tank while it fills. Often the seat simply needs cleaning.

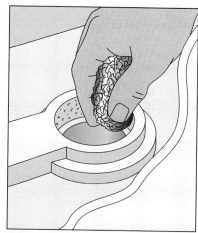

NOTE: *Shut off the water to the tank, and flush the toilet to get the water out.* Check the tank ball or flapper. If it has gunk on it, wipe it clean and smooth, using an abrasive pad. Once it's cleaned, feel the valve seat to see if it is pitted or corroded if it's metal. Flexible seats can be pried out and replaced. If you have a damaged metal seat, replace the entire flush valve.

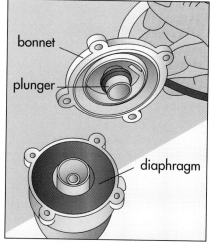

Repair a diaphragm ballcock.
NOTE: *Shut off the water, and flush the toilet.* Remove the four screws on top of the ballcock, and lift off the bonnet. Clean out any deposits. Replace any worn parts, including the plunger. If a number of parts look worn, replace the entire ballcock.

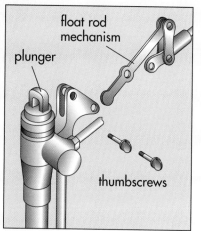

Repair a plunger ballcock.
NOTE: *Shut off the water, and flush the toilet.* This is the oldest type of ballcock, and there are a number of parts that can go bad. You may need to replace it with either a diaphragm or float-cup ballcock. But first try cleaning and replacing the washers.

Remove the thumbscrews holding the float rod mechanism

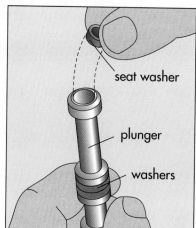

in place, then lift it out and set it aside. Remove the plunger by pulling up on it. Typically, you'll find a seat washer as well as a couple of other washers. (In very old models, you may even find leather washers.) Remove and replace all of the washers, reassemble the mechanism, and turn the water back on.

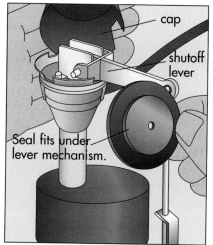

Repair a float-cup ballcock.
NOTE: *Shut off the water, and flush the toilet.* This is the newest and the simplest design, and it rarely acts up. Pry off the cap, then remove the bonnet by lifting the lever on the float rod mechanism, pushing the mechanism down, and twisting counterclockwise firmly. Clean out any gunk, and replace the seal if it looks worn.

FIXING LEAKY TANKS AND BOWLS

A puddle of water on the floor near the toilet can be fixed in several ways. On a hot, humid day, condensation dripping from the cool outside of the tank or bowl could be substantial enough to make a puddle. You can simply live with it or install rigid-foam tank insulation.

A chronic leak probably means a faulty water supply connection, spud gasket, or wax ring. Often you simply need to tighten the hold-down bolts to solve the problem. A crack in a tank can sometimes be patched from the inside with silicone sealant. A cracked bowl should be replaced.

YOU'LL NEED...
TIME: About two hours to replace a spud gasket or a wax ring.
SKILLS: No special skills, but be careful not to crack the toilet.
TOOLS: Wrenches, screwdriver, putty knife.

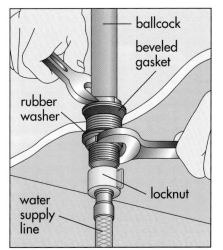

A leak at the water supply line
If the leak comes from where the water supply enters the tank, first tighten the locknut. If that doesn't work, shut off the water, flush the toilet, and sponge out the water that remains in the tank. Disconnect the water supply line, remove the locknut, and replace the old beveled gasket and rubber washer with new ones.

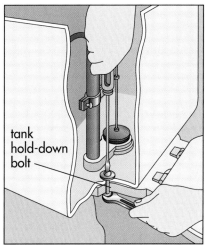

A leak between the tank and bowl
Extended use can cause the tank hold-down bolts to loosen enough to produce a leak at the spud gasket. Use a screwdriver and a wrench to tighten the bolts to squeeze the tank against the spud gasket. If the leak persists, shut off the water, flush, and sponge out any water. Detach the supply line, remove the hold-down bolts, lift out the tank, and replace the spud gasket (see page 56). Reassemble.

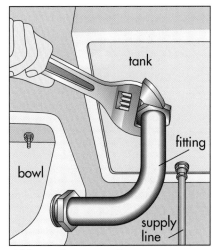

Older-style connections
With some old toilets, the tank connects to the bowl with a fitting. If leaks develop at either end of the fitting, tightening the nuts may stop the leak. If not, take the toilet apart, and replace any worn parts at a plumbing supply source.

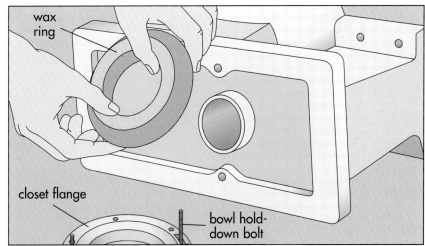

A leak at the base of the bowl
If the bowl is cracked, you'll have to replace it. If the bowl is sound, try gently tightening the hold-down nuts (see page 56). If that doesn't stop the leak, replace the wax ring. Begin by shutting off the water, flushing the toilet, and sponging out any remaining water.

Disconnect the water supply line, and remove the nuts on the hold-down bolts. Lift out the toilet. Scrape away the old wax ring and any old putty on the bottom of the bowl. Press a new wax ring in place according to the manufacturer's directions. Reinstall the toilet (see page 56).

REPLACING TOILETS

Replacing a toilet is surprisingly easy. Problems arise only if the closet flange isn't at the floor surface (see below) or if the floor isn't level (shim the toilet after you set it on the hold-down bolts).

Toilets are ceramic, so work carefully. It is possible to crack a toilet if you bang it or screw down a nut too hard. Most toilets sold today have their drains centered 12 inches from the back wall. Measure yours from the wall to the hold-down bolt. If yours is centered 10 inches from the wall, either buy a 10-inch toilet or install a special offset closet flange. If you need to run supply and drain lines for a new installation, see pages 82–89.

YOU'LL NEED...

TIME: Three hours to remove an old toilet and install a new one.
SKILLS: No special skills needed—just work carefully.
TOOLS: Wrenches, screwdriver, hacksaw, tongue-and-groove pliers, putty knife.

EXPERTS' INSIGHT

IF THE FLANGE IS LOW

If your bathroom has a new layer of flooring, the closet flange often will end up below the floor surface. In that case, a regular wax ring may not be thick enough to seal the toilet bowl to the flange. You can extend the ring upward with a special flange extender (see page 57) or double the wax ring. Place a wax ring without a plastic flange on the toilet, then place a flanged ring on top of it.

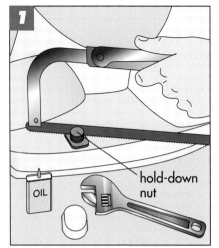

1. Remove the old toilet.
Note: *Shut off the water.*
Flush the toilet, and remove remaining water with a sponge. Disconnect the water supply line, and unscrew the hold-down nuts. Often these are rusted tight. If penetrating oil does not loosen them, cut the nuts with a hacksaw. Lift the toilet out.

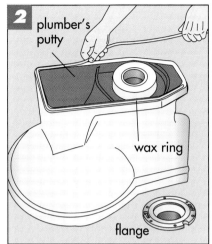

2. Prepare the new toilet bowl.
Carefully remove the new toilet bowl from its container, and turn it upside down on a cushioned surface, such as a throw rug or folded drop cloth. Run a rope of plumber's putty around the perimeter of the bowl's base, and fit a wax ring (sold separately) over the outlet opening.

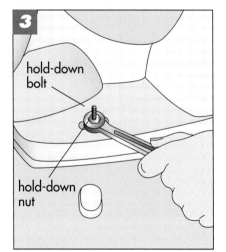

3. Install the bowl.
Return the bowl to its upright position, and gently set it in place atop the closet flange. Make sure the hold-down bolts align with the holes in the base. Press down on the bowl with both hands, and align it. Slip a metal washer and a nut over each bolt, and tighten slowly. Don't overtighten or you could crack the bowl.

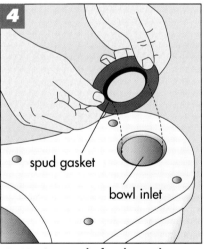

4. You're ready for the tank.
First, lay the spud gasket, beveled side down, over the bowl inlet opening. This forms the seal between the tank and the bowl. Or, slip the spud gasket onto the threaded tailpiece located at the bottom of the tank if you have the older-style connectors shown on page 55.

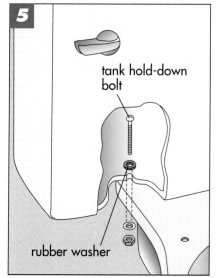

5. Install the tank.

Gently lower the tank onto the bowl, aligning the tank holes with those toward the rear of the bowl. Secure the tank to the bowl with the hold-down bolts, washers, and nuts provided with the toilet. Be sure that the rubber washer goes inside the tank under the bolt.

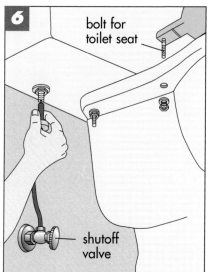

6. Attach water supply.

Complete the installation by hooking up the water supply line. The easiest way is to use a flexible plastic or chrome-braided supply line. Or use chrome-finished flexible copper tubing and compression fittings (see page 22).

Money $ Saver

WATER-SAVING TOILETS

In most localities, toilets that use only 1.6 gallons of water are required for new installations. These save money by reducing water consumption, but they do not flush strongly. They differ from older models by having a smaller tank or a mechanism that restricts the amount of water in the tank.

Don't buy a new toilet simply to save money in water use. Reduce an old toilet's consumption by setting a brick into the tank or by bending the float ball's rod so the ball sits lower in the tank. Most people don't mind the reduced flushing power of new models. If it is a problem for you, get a pressure-assisted toilet.

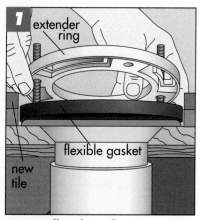

1. Install a closet flange extender.

If your floor surface is more than half an inch above the closet flange (as will happen when you install new tile), you must extend the flange so it's flush with the floor. A closet flange extender with flexible gaskets and a plastic extender ring make up the difference. First, clean off old wax, insert new bolts, and slip on a flexible gasket and the extender ring.

2. Make a waxless seal.

The closet flange extender should fit flush with the surface of your new flooring. (If it does not, add an additional extender ring.) Add the second flexible gasket. This gasket takes the place of the wax ring. Most kits also include handy plastic shims for leveling the toilet once it is placed on the hold-down bolts. See page 56 for completing the bowl installation.

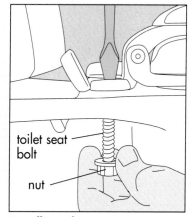

Install a toilet seat.

To remove an old toilet seat, lower the seat and cover, and pry up the little lids that cover the toilet seat bolts. Hold the nut from below, unscrew the bolts, and lift out the seat.

Clean out the area around the bolt holes, and install the new seat by aligning the seat with the holes and installing the bolts. Screw nuts onto the bolts, and tighten the bolts just enough to firmly hold the seat.

MAINTAINING AND FIXING WATER HEATERS

Water heaters are little more than giant insulated water bottles with heaters. As hot water is used, cold water enters through a dip tube. This lowers the water temperature inside the tank, causing a thermostat to call for heat. In gas units, burners beneath the water tank kick in and continue heating the water until the desired temperature is reached. Heating elements perform the same function in electric water heaters. Most water heater problems are the result of sediment buildup or rust. You can help prevent this by opening the drain valve every few months and flushing out a few gallons of water. This purges rust and other buildup from the heater.

YOU'LL NEED...

TIME: Allow two hours for inspection and minor repairs.
SKILLS: No special skills needed.
TOOLS: Crescent wrench, tongue-and-groove pliers.

MEASUREMENTS

VITAL NUMBERS

The nameplate on the outside of your water heater gives the unit's vital statistics. Look for:

■ **Tank Capacity:** The more gallons it holds, the less chance you'll run out of hot water during a shower. A 40-gallon tank suits most households.

■ **R-Value:** The better insulated the unit is, the more efficient it will be. If yours has an R-value of less than 7, wrap the tank with insulation.

■ **Installation Clearances:** This tells you how much room you must leave between the unit and any combustible materials.

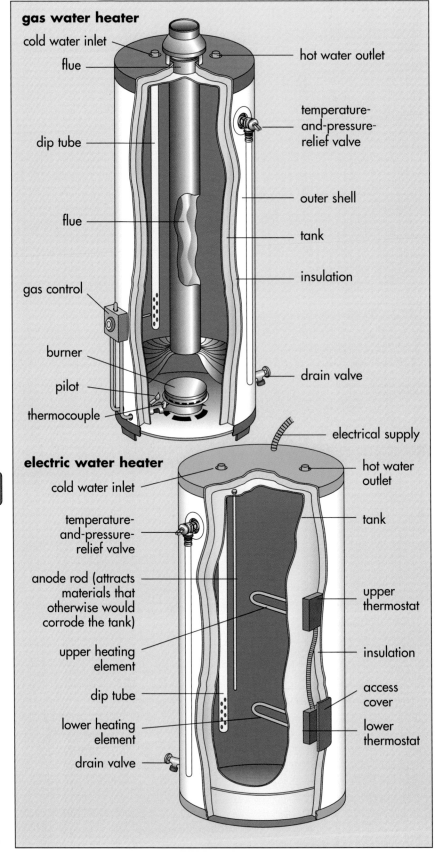

gas water heater
- cold water inlet
- flue
- dip tube
- flue
- gas control
- burner
- pilot
- thermocouple
- hot water outlet
- temperature-and-pressure-relief valve
- outer shell
- tank
- insulation
- drain valve

electric water heater
- cold water inlet
- temperature-and-pressure-relief valve
- anode rod (attracts materials that otherwise would corrode the tank)
- upper heating element
- dip tube
- lower heating element
- drain valve
- electrical supply
- hot water outlet
- tank
- upper thermostat
- insulation
- access cover
- lower thermostat

WATER HEATER REPAIR CHART

Symptom	Cause	Repair
No hot water.	No power to the heater (electric). Pilot light out (gas).	Check circuit breaker or fuse (electric). Relight pilot; replace thermocouple if pilot does not stay lit.
Water not hot enough.	Upper element burned out (electric).	Replace upper element.
Not enough hot water—hot water runs out quickly.	Thermostat set too low. Hot water must travel a long way to get to faucets. Sediment buildup in tank. Lower element burned out (electric). Burner blocked by dirt (gas). Leaking faucets. Tank not large enough for demand.	Turn thermostat up. Insulate hot water pipes (see page 32). Drain and refill tank. Replace lower element. Clean burner, or call gas company. Repair faucets. Replace with a larger tank.
Tank makes noise.	Sediment in tank.	Drain and refill tank.
Leak from temperature-and-pressure-relief valve.	Thermostat set too high. Defective temperature-and-pressure-relief valve.	Lower thermostat setting. Replace valve.
Leak around tank base.	Tank corrosion has created a leak.	Replace water heater.

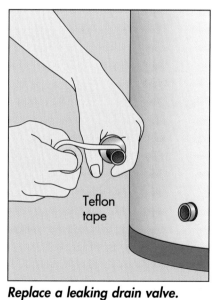

Replace a leaking drain valve.
If your water heater's drain valve leaks, shut off the cold water stop valve, shut off the gas or the electrical current, and drain the water heater. Unscrew the faulty valve. Apply Teflon tape or pipe joint compound to the male threads of a new valve, and install. Fill tank, and restore power or gas.

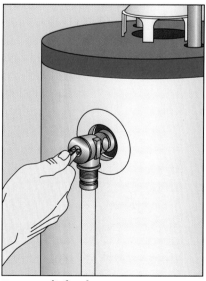

Test a relief valve.
Either on top or high on the side of the water heater, you'll find a relief valve that opens if the temperature or pressure in the tank gets too high. (Thus, it is called a "T-and-P-relief valve.") Test it once a year by pulling on the handle; if water rushes out of the pipe attached to it, all is well.

Replace a faulty relief valve.
If no water comes out, replace it. Shut off the cold water, turn off power or gas to the unit, and drain some of the water. Remove the attached drainpipe and the valve. Apply Teflon tape or pipe joint compound to the male threads when you install the new valve.

REPAIRING ELECTRIC WATER HEATERS

If you are not getting enough hot water, make sure the thermostat is set correctly. Also drain the heater if you suspect it is filled with sediment. If you have no hot water, check for power to the unit. If none of these measures solves the problem, you need to replace the thermostats and heating elements. To determine which thermostat and element to replace, see the Experts' Insight below.

YOU'LL NEED...

TIME: About two hours.
SKILLS: Making electrical connections.
TOOLS: Screwdriver, tongue-and-groove pliers, neon circuit tester.

CAUTION!

DANGER! HIGH VOLTAGE!
Electric water heaters use 240-volt current, twice the amount used in a normal receptacle. Be sure to remove the fuse or shut off the breaker at the service panel. Test wires for electricity before disassembling anything.

EXPERTS' INSIGHT

WHICH TO REPLACE?

Electric water heaters have two thermostats and heating elements (see page 58). To find out which pair is defective, turn on a hot water faucet. If the water gets warm but not hot, the upper thermostat and element are the culprits and should be replaced. If the water is hot for awhile then goes cold, replace the lower element and thermostat.

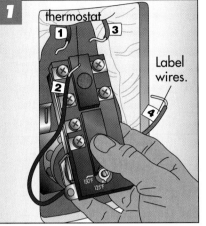

1. Remove the thermostat.
Note: *Shut off the power, shut off the water to the heater, and drain the heater.* Remove the cover plate, and use a neon circuit tester to make sure the power is off. Drain the water heater (see page 62). Push aside insulation, label and disconnect the wires, and remove the thermostat.

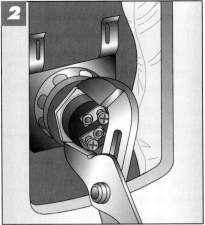

2. Remove the element.
Use tongue-and-groove pliers to unscrew the element, then pull it out. Remove the gasket if there is one. Take the old element and thermostat with you to your supplier to make sure you get the correct replacement.

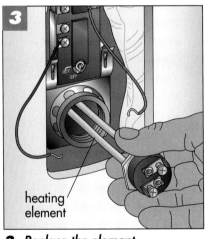

3. Replace the element.
If the replacement element has a gasket, coat both sides of the gasket with pipe joint compound, and slide the gasket onto the new element. Slide the element in, and screw it in place. Tighten with tongue-and-groove pliers.

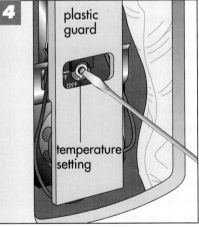

4. Install, set the thermostat.
Slide the new thermostat into place, and reconnect the wires, using your labels as guides. Snap in the plastic guard. Use a screwdriver to set the thermostat. Press the red reset button on the thermostat. Make sure the drain valve is closed, and turn on the shutoff valve to fill the tank. When water flows to your hot water faucets, turn off the faucets, and restore electrical power.

REPAIRING GAS WATER HEATERS

*I*f you suddenly lose hot water, or if your unit is not heating water efficiently, remove the access panel at the bottom of your water heater and check the pilot light. If it's not burning, relight it according to directions printed on the unit. If it won't relight, you need a new thermocouple. If you have yellow rather than blue flame, you need to replace the thermocouple and/or clean the burner. If you smell smoke or fumes, check your flue immediately.

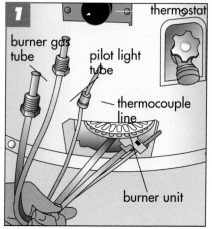

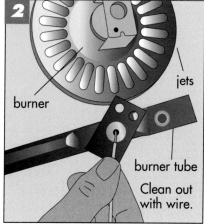

1. Remove the burner unit.
Note: *Shut off the gas.* If you need to replace a thermocouple or clean the burner, first remove the burner unit. Disconnect the pilot light tube, the burner gas tube, and the thermocouple line. Pull down on the tubes, and carefully pull the entire burner unit out.

2. Clean the burner and tube.
Turn the burner counterclockwise to unscrew it from the tube. With a thin piece of wire, clean out the small orifice at the point where the tube enters the burner. Also use wire to clean the small orifice in the pilot light tube. Use a vacuum cleaner to suck out any rust and debris from the burner jets and inside the burner area of the unit.

YOU'LL NEED...

TIME: An hour or two for any of the operations on this page.
SKILLS: Handling compression fittings on gas tubes.
TOOLS: Wrench or pliers, thin wire, small wire brush, vacuum cleaner.

EXPERTS' INSIGHT

REGULAR MAINTENANCE FOR YOUR GAS WATER HEATER

■ To avoid the dangerous buildup of fumes from a faulty flue, check your flue at least once a year. Be sure it is efficiently pulling fumes out of your house (see Step 4). To dismantle the flue to check for debris, see page 62.

■ Once a year, or at least whenever you replace the thermocouple, clean the burner, even if it shows no symptoms of being clogged. A clean burner will burn more efficiently and help your water heater last longer.

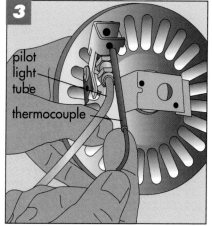

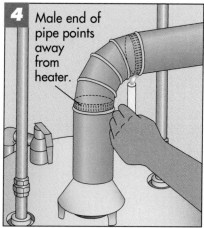

3. Replace a thermocouple.
If your pilot light won't light or is not staying lit, pull the old thermocouple from its bracket. Take it to your supplier to get one exactly like it. Push the new one into place until it clicks tight. The tip of the thermocouple should be right next to the end of the pilot gas tube so the pilot flame will touch it.

4. Maintain the flue.
A rusted, clogged, or loose-fitting flue will cause harmful fumes to enter your home. To check to see if the flue is drawing, light a piece of paper, and blow it out. While it is smoking, hold it near the opening at the bottom of the flue. If the smoke is not sucked out, your flue needs cleaning. Also check for leaks by holding a candle near openings. If the flame is drawn, tighten the joint.

REPLACING GAS WATER HEATERS

Though water heaters sometimes last 25 years or more, they usually give out sooner—the victims of rust and sediment. When yours fails, there's no need to call in a plumber. Though it may seem like a complicated job, installing a gas water heater involves only two or three pipe hookups, and an electric heater requires connecting some wires. Removing the old unit is often the most difficult part of the job.

First, make sure your old water heater can't be fixed. If the tank itself leaks—not the pipes—the lining has rusted and the heater must be replaced. If your heater is not producing enough hot water, it may simply be suffering from a buildup of rust and sediment, which insulates the water from the burner and forces it to work more

often to satisfy demand. Drain the heater. You may be able to flush out enough sediment to make it efficient. If it still produces too little hot water, replace it.

YOU'LL NEED...

TIME: Allow a day to remove the old heater and install the new.
SKILLS: Basic plumbing skills.
TOOLS: Wrenches for loosening unions or flexible fittings, garden hose, level, dolly, screwdriver.

CAUTION!
PRECAUTIONS WITH GAS
If you do not have a gas shutoff near the water heater, shut off the gas to your house by turning the valve on the gas meter with a large wrench. If you do this, be sure to relight all the pilot lights in your house after you turn the gas back on.

EXPERTS' INSIGHT

CHOOSING THE RIGHT WATER HEATER

■ Check the nameplate on the old unit, and note its capacity. You'll be safe purchasing a new one of the same size, unless you have recently installed or plan to buy an appliance that consumes a lot of hot water, such as a dishwasher. Usually, a 30- to 50-gallon unit will have enough capacity for an average home.
■ Units designed to heat water quickly, called fast recovery units, are more expensive to buy and operate, but they handle peak demand times better. Standard units don't heat as fast but are more economical to run.
■ If you have hard water, consider a unit with an extra anode for collecting mineral deposits (see the drawing on page 58).

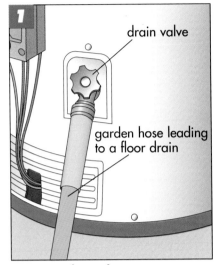

1. Drain the tank.
NOTE: *Shut off the main water valve to your house, and shut off the gas at the heater.* Drain the water lines in your home by opening hot and cold taps in an upstairs faucet. Also open both taps positioned closest to the system's lowest point. Attach a garden hose to the water heater drain valve, open the valve, and drain the tank.

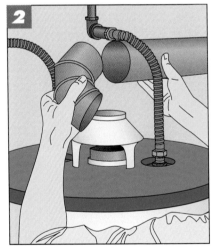

2. Dismantle the flue.
Remove the sheet-metal screws, and dismantle enough ductwork to give yourself room to work. Keep track of which piece of ductwork goes where, and be careful not to bend it.

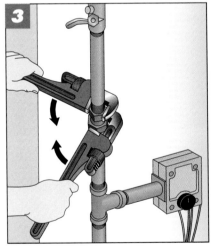

3. Disconnect the gas line.
Many localities require that gas line be rigid pipe all the way to the water heater; others allow you to use a flexible gas line. Take apart a gas line union (as shown), or disconnect the flexible line.

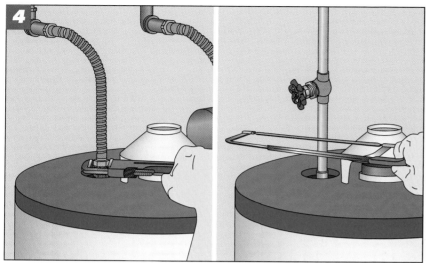

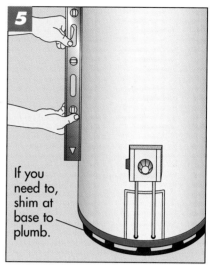

4. Disconnect the water lines.
Mark hot and cold water lines so you won't hook up the new heater backward. If you have galvanized pipe, open unions near the unit. If you have rigid copper, cut the pipe with a hacksaw or tubing cutter just below the shutoff valves. Make the cuts straight, so you can tap into the lines easily with new soldered pipe or flexible water lines when you install the new heater. If you have flexible lines, disconnect them. Move the old unit out with an appliance dolly.

CAUTION!
IT MAY BE HEAVY!
If sediment buildup clogged your old heater, it will be extremely heavy. Have a helper and a good appliance dolly, and take care not to strain your back.

5. Set the new unit in place.
Move the new water heater into place. Position it to make your gas connection as easy as possible. Check for plumb and level, shimming if necessary. If the unit is in an area prone to dampness, purchase a traylike base to protect it.

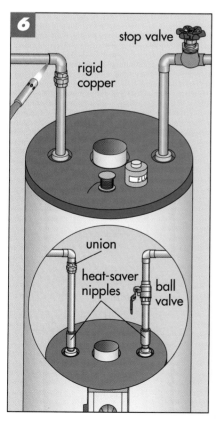

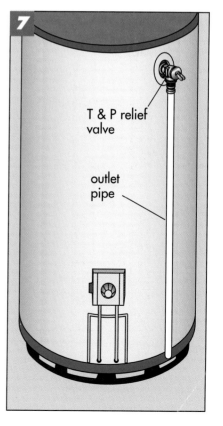

6. Connect the water lines.
Find out code requirements for the water lines. If they're permitted, flexible copper water connectors are usually the easiest way to go. Otherwise, solder rigid copper, or install galvanized pipe with a union. To save energy, install heat-saver nipples at each inlet. These temperature-sensitive in-line valves hold back water until it's needed. Follow directions, installing the cold water nipple with the arrow pointing down, the hot water nipple with the arrow pointing up.

7. Install T & P relief valve.
You may have to purchase a temperature-and-pressure-relief valve separately. Be sure it matches the working-pressure rating of the tank, as given on the nameplate. Wrap the threads with Teflon tape, and screw the valve in—either on top or near the top on the side.

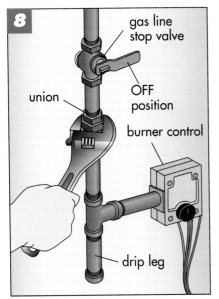

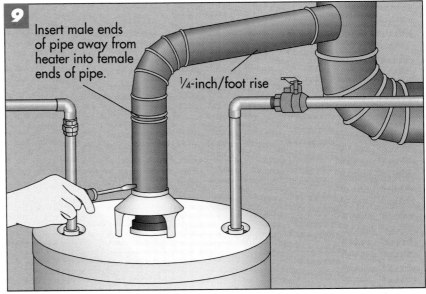

8. Hook up the gas.

Connect a gas (black pipe) nipple to the burner control of the water heater, and connect the nipple to the gas line. Be sure to install a drip leg to collect sediment and moisture from the gas line.

9. Install the flue.

If your old flue worked well and your new water heater is the same height as the old one, you can reuse the old flue. Make sure it isn't blocked. Clean out any dust, rust, or sediment from the flue. If you replace or add to the vent, use galvanized pipe fittings that are designed for venting gas. When running a horizontal section, maintain at least a ¼-inch-per-foot rise. Insert male ends of the vent into female ends away from the water heater so the fumes will not have a chance to escape. Fasten each joint of the vent with two sheet-metal screws.

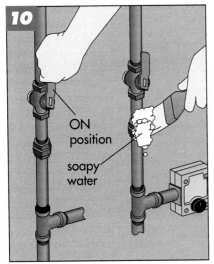

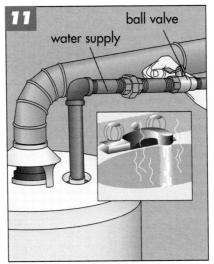

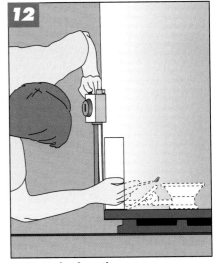

10. Check for gas leaks.

Open the gas stop valve. Test for leaks by brushing soapy water on all the connections. Watch for bubbles. If you see any, tighten the connection. If they persist, shut off the gas, disassemble, carefully clean the threads, and start again.

11. Turn on the water.

Open the water supply valve. Open the nearest hot faucet about halfway, and allow the system to "bleed." First, air will come out, then the spattering of water mixed with air. When the water flows freely, close the faucet.

12. Light the pilot.

Open the access panel at the bottom of the tank, and light the pilot according to the directions printed on the water heater. Adjust the temperature setting.

REPLACING ELECTRIC WATER HEATERS

Installing an electric water heater is similar to installing a gas unit. The differences are that you make electrical rather than gas connections, and there is no flue on an electric water heater.

YOU'LL NEED...

TIME About a day.
SKILLS: Making electrical and plumbing connections.
TOOLS: Wrenches for unions or flexible fittings, garden hose for draining, level, appliance dolly, screwdriver, neon tester.

CAUTION!

DANGER! HIGH VOLTAGE!
Working with 240-volt circuits is a serious matter. Remove the fuse or turn off the circuit breaker, and check to make sure the power is off.

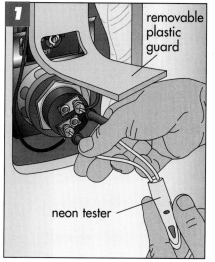

removable plastic guard

neon tester

1. Remove the panel and test.
NOTE: *Shut off the power and water.* Remove the access panel for the thermostat (usually behind the lower panel), push aside any insulation, and lift or remove the plastic guard. Test for current with a neon tester to make sure you have turned off the circuit.

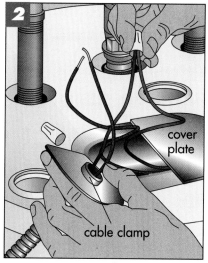

cover plate

cable clamp

2. Disconnect, mark wires.
Remove the electrical cover plate at the side or the top of the unit. Disconnect the wires, and mark them with pieces of tape so you'll know exactly where to attach them on the new unit. Loosen the screw on the cable clamp, and carefully pull the cable out.

Complete steps 1, 4, and 5 on pages 62–63.

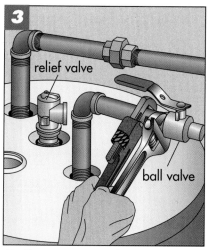

relief valve

ball valve

3. Connect water pipes.
Install water lines (see page 63). Supply lines can be galvanized steel pipe (see pages 24–25), rigid copper (see pages 18–19), or flexible water connectors (see pages 62–63). Install a ball valve on the supply line (see page 30). Install a relief valve, and attach an outlet pipe (see page 63).

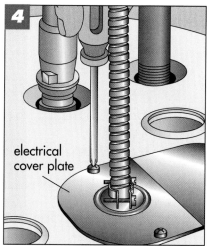

electrical cover plate

4. Make the electrical connections.
Remove the electrical cover plate. Run the cable through the clamp. Connect the black and white wires with wire connectors, and attach the ground wire to the ground screw. Tighten the screw on the clamp to hold the cable in place, gently push the wires inside, and replace the cover plate.

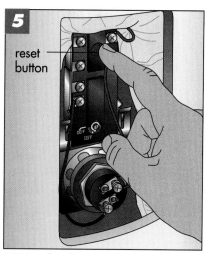

reset button

5. Set the thermostat.
Set the water heater to the temperature you want. Press the reset button, and replace the plastic guard, insulation, and access panels. Turn the water on as shown in Step 11 on page 64.

REPAIRING TUB AND SHOWER CONTROLS

Tub and shower controls work much the same way as sink faucets, so repairing them involves many of the same operations, except you are working horizontally rather than vertically. Also, tub and shower controls are a bit more complicated, because in addition to mixing hot and cold water, they must divert water either to the tub spout or to the showerhead. The anatomy drawings on these pages show the inner workings of common types.

Sometimes the parts are hard to get at. You may have to chip away at tiles in order to get your tools to the shower control parts.

If a shower control body is damaged and needs to be replaced, look at the other side of the wall to see if you have an access panel. If so, you may be able to work from behind and minimize damage to your shower wall. Usually, replacing a shower control body means tearing up a shower wall and retiling.

YOU'LL NEED...

TIME: About two hours for most repairs, not including time spent looking for parts.
SKILLS: Basic plumbing skills and ability to work with tile.
TOOLS: Screwdriver, pliers, wrenches.

Note: *Be sure to shut off the supply stop valves, built-in shutoff valves, or the main water valve before making these repairs.*

Two-handle control

The handles on these usually contain stems with washers. Each washer presses against a seat in order to shut the water off (see pages 36–39). To stop a drip, shut off the water, and remove the stem—you may have to use a special stem wrench or a deep socket, or chip away at the tiles to get at the packing nut. Replace the washer and the seat, if necessary, just as you would on a sink faucet (see page 37). If the diverter valve on the spout is not working properly, replace the spout.

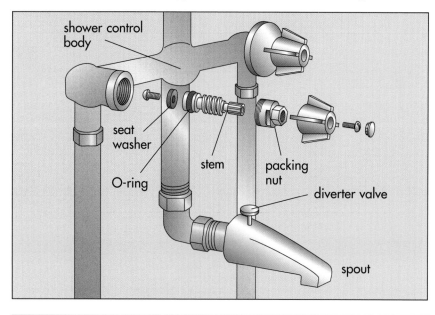

Three-handle control

This type is much like a two-handle control, but it has a central handle that controls a diverter valve. The valve directs water either up or down—out the showerhead or out the spout. If the diverter valve sticks, or if it does not completely divert water to either the showerhead or to the spout, shut off the water, and remove it just as you would a regular stem (see page 37). Take it apart, clean it, and replace any washers or O-rings (see pages 37–39). Or, replace the whole stem with a new one.

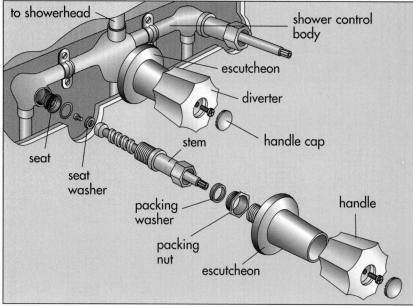

One-handle ball control

This type has seals and springs like ball-type sink faucets, so repairs are similar to those shown on pages 42–43. As the handle is raised, the ball rotates in such a way that its openings begin to align with the supply line ports, allowing water to pass through the ball and out the spout.

Impeded flow is usually the result of clogged orifices or worn seals. Shut the water off, and remove the ball—a few ball controls have setscrews that you may have to remove to do this. Clean out the orifices, replace any worn rubber parts, and lubricate them with heatproof grease.

While you have the faucet apart, check the ball for wear and corrosion. If it's worn, replace it with a new one.

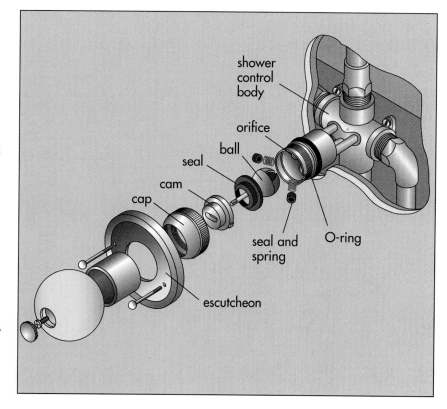

One-handle cartridge control

There are other configurations of one-handled cartridge controls besides the one shown here, so you may have to search out the location of your parts, such as the retaining clip. Parts are usually made of plastic; be careful not to crack them.

To repair a leak or limited flow, remove the handle, unscrew the retainer nut, and pull out the cartridge. Clean away any deposits, and replace worn rubber or plastic parts. Lubricate all rubber parts with heatproof grease. Or, simply replace the cartridge itself. When you replace the cartridge, be sure to note its original position, and insert the new one the same way. If you don't, your hot and cold water will be reversed.

See pages 40–41 for more on repairing cartridge faucets.

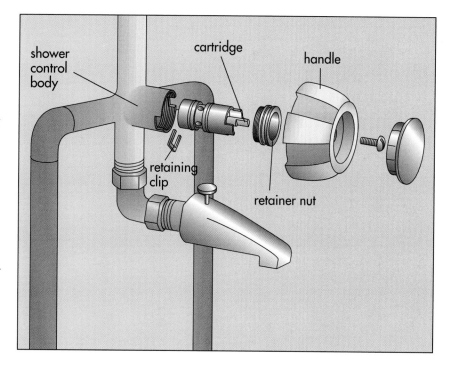

REPLACING BATHTUBS

This is a difficult, time-consuming job, but it's within the reach of a do-it-yourselfer who plans carefully and takes the time to do it right. You will need a helper. In most cases, the wall repair is just as much work as the tub installation and plumbing. Visit your local library to find books specifically about wall finishing and tiling.

YOU'LL NEED...

TIME: Several days to remove an old tub, install a new one, and fix the walls.
SKILLS: Basic plumbing skills, wall-finishing skills.
TOOLS: Screwdriver, channel-type pliers, prying bars, hammer and chisel, carpentry and wall-preparation tools.

EXPERTS' INSIGHT

CHOOSING A TUB

■ Most tubs are 60 inches long, but 54- and 66-inch ones are available. Make sure you get a size that fits your space. Widths vary, too. This can result in a gap between the new tub and the floor tile. You may have to add some tiles, or even build the wall out with a layer or two of cement board or green drywall. This could spare you retiling the entire bathroom floor.
■ Cast-iron is the most durable but also the most expensive and heaviest tub material. Fiberglass is convenient but will scratch. Baked-enamel steel tubs are fairly light and durable, but they can chip, and they are noisy when being filled.

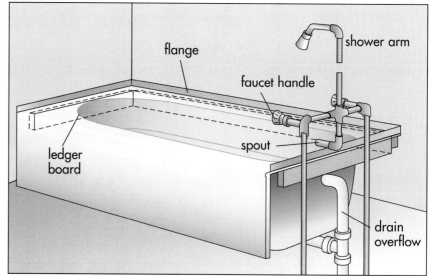

Tub installation overview
The supply system for a tub and shower includes a faucet (for possible types, see pages 66–67), a spout, and a showerhead and arm. In most cases, these do not need to be disturbed when you remove and replace a tub. (Sometimes you need to remove the spout and handles to get the old tub out.)

Remove the drain assembly, and detach the drain overflow to remove the tub. When you replace the tub, replace the drain assembly as well. You can choose one that has a trip lever at the top to control the drain stopper, or choose a simpler model in which you control the drain at the stopper (see page 78).

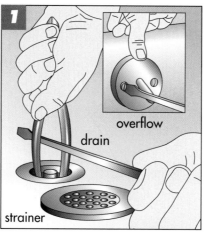

1. Disconnect the drain.
Loosen the screws, and remove the overflow plate. Pull out the trip lever and linkage (see page 78). Remove the strainer, and use a pair of pliers and a screwdriver to unscrew the drain piece. You may have to pull out the stopper with pieces of linkage attached to it.

2. Cut the wall away.
Chisel into the grout, and pry out at least one course of tile along the edge of the tub. Cut away as much of the wall as necessary to reveal the tub flange and to get at any screws or nails that fasten the flange to the wall.

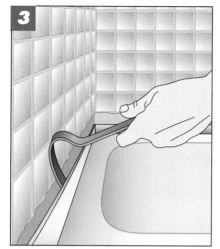

3. Remove the tub.

Depending on how it was installed, you may be able simply to pry the tub loose, or you might have to pull nails, unfasten screws, or disconnect clips that secure the tub to the wall. Pull the tub away from the wall, and remove it. (See the box for removal tips.)

2×4 ledger board

4. Prepare for the new tub.

Consult manufacturer's directions for any special installation preparations. For a cast-iron tub, install a 2×4 ledger board, shown above. For steel or fiberglass, use the screws or clips provided with the unit. Some fiberglass bathtubs are installed in a bed of mortar to add support.

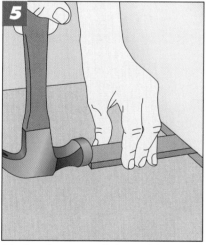

5. Set the new tub in position.

Attach a new drain assembly, or check to see that the old one will fit. Slide the new tub into place, reversing whatever procedures you used to remove the old one. Check for level along its length and across its width, and shim if necessary.

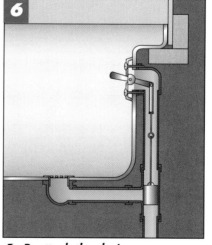

6. Reattach the drain.

Chances are, you will need to have access to the drain either from below or from behind. Align the overflow and the drain with their holes. Apply plumber's putty to the threads of the drain piece. Attach the overflow plate and the drain piece, and fasten them in place, taking care not to scratch the chrome surfaces.

EXPERTS' INSIGHT

REMOVING OLD TUBS

■ Depending on the layout of your bathroom, you might be able to tilt the tub in one piece and carry it out the door. Have at least one helper on hand.

■ In some situations, the only solution is to cut a hole in a wall without any obstructing plumbing, and slide the tub through into the next room. This is not as drastic as it sounds: You will only have to cut one or two studs, and the wall patching may actually be less than you would have with other methods of removal.

■ If the tub is cast-iron, by far the easiest way to remove it is to break it apart with a sledgehammer. Wear protective eyewear and work gloves. Remove or cover any items in the bathroom that might be scratched.

Money $ Saver

WALL-FINISHING OPTIONS

■ You may not have to tear out all of your tiles and retile the entire tub surround. If you work carefully, you can piece in cement board or green drywall (see page 95) in the places where you cut away the wall. You can then fill in the space with tiles.

■ Other good options include acrylic and fiberglass panels. These are reasonably priced, and they can be installed in a fraction of the time it takes to tile and grout.

OPENING CLOGGED DRAINS

Sooner or later, every homeowner encounters a clogged drain. If you hire a professional to clear it out, you will usually get a better price if you call someone who specializes in clearing drains, rather than a general plumber. But it will still cost you plenty; a professional's time costs the same whether the job requires something highly specialized or something you could have done yourself.

Most clogs are not due to faulty plumbing but to the slow buildup of solids that sink drains aren't intended to cope with. Only toilets are plumbed to handle solid waste; sinks, tubs, and showers have drains designed to carry away water only. Hair, grease, soap, food scraps, and gunk will clog up a drain. With a few basic tools, you can clear most clogs and get the system flowing again.

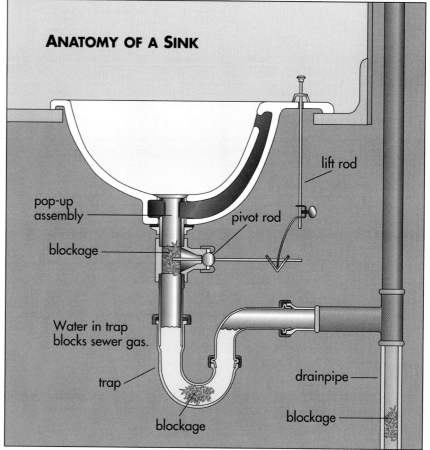

ANATOMY OF A SINK

lift rod

pop-up assembly

pivot rod

blockage

Water in trap blocks sewer gas.

trap

blockage

drainpipe

blockage

TOOLS TO USE

POWER AUGERS

■ For extra augering power, rent or buy a power auger or an augering attachment for a drill. The drill attachment is less expensive but not as sturdy as a power auger.

■ A high-quality tool will have a second cable that runs through the middle of the wound-wire augering cable. This keeps the auger cable from kinking, and it allows you to retrieve the auger cable if it should break. If your auger does not have this second cable and it breaks—a real possibility, especially if you are doing heavy-duty augering—you'll have a length of auger cable stuck in your pipe.

Where clogs happen
The slow buildup of soapy slime inside a drainpipe, a point of resistance such as a drain assembly, or a sharp bend in the drain can cause a clog. If a fixture is often clogged, install a strainer to keep solids from going down the drain. It will be well worth cleaning the strainer occasionally.

EXPERTS' INSIGHT

USING DRAIN CLEANERS

■ If your drain is completely stopped up and water is not moving through it at all, do not use a drain cleaner. It will not help the problem, and some types will actually harden if they cannot get through, making the clog worse. Drain cleaner can damage pipes, and it might splash you when you plunge or auger the drain.

■ If your drain is sluggish, use only nonacid drain cleaners (sodium hydroxide and copper sulfide are safe). Pour them in when the drain is sluggish, not when it is completely stopped. Regular use of a drain cleaner can keep the pipes clear of hair, soap, grease, and so on.

■ To maintain a smooth-flowing drain, every week or so run very hot water into the drain for a minute or two. This will clear away small amounts of grease and soap and keep them from building up.

USING SIMPLE UNCLOGGING METHODS

When a sink clogs up, first figure out where the blockage might be. It could be anywhere along the three main sections of a household drain system: in the fixture drain, in the drain stack that serves multiple fixtures, or in the main sewer line that carries waste out of the house (see page 8). Usually the problem will be close to a fixture, because the drain pipe and trap near a fixture are narrower than the stack and main sewer lines they tie into. To verify that the clog is near the fixture, check other drains in your home. If more than one won't clear, something is stuck in a drain stack. If no drains work, the problem is farther down the line, probably in the main sewer line.

YOU'LL NEED...

TIME: An hour or two to perform the operations shown.
SKILLS: No special skills needed.
TOOLS: Screwdriver, auger, plunger.

EXPERTS' INSIGHT

PLUNGING SINKS WITH MORE THAN ONE DRAIN

■ When plunging a double sink, it's best to have a helper block up one of the drain holes by pressing a wet rag firmly into it, while you plunge the other drain hole.

■ A dishwasher drains through a hose into the disposal or the sink plumbing (see page 104). Before plunging, use a C-clamp and two wood blocks to seal the drain hose and keep water from backing into the dishwasher.

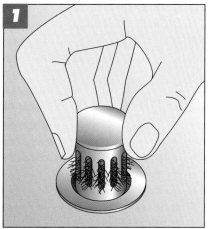

1. Clean the strainer.
Clearing a sink may involve nothing more than removing the strainer or stopper from the drain opening. Push the stopper up, and pull away any soap, hair, food matter, or other debris that may clog the opening, or be dangling down into the drain.

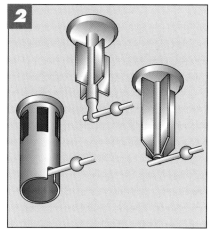

2. Detach the pop-up assembly.
The strainers in kitchen sinks and many bathroom sinks simply lift out. Others require a slight turn before they will come out. With some, you must pull out the pivot rod before the stopper will come out. If you want to auger the sink, you will have to remove the pivot rod (see below and page 78).

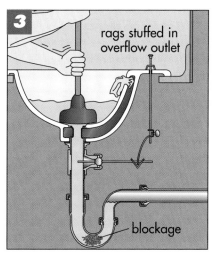

3. Plunge a sink.
A plunger uses water pressure to blast out obstructions and suction to bring stuff up. The plunger's rubber cup must seal tightly around the drain opening. Water in the sink helps create a seal; rubbing petroleum jelly on the plunger rim also helps. Stuff a rag into any openings, such as an overflow outlet. Push and pull rapidly with the plunger.

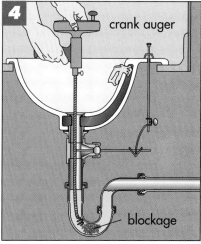

4. Auger a sink.
If plunging doesn't work, fit an auger down the drain. Cranking the auger handle rotates a stiff spring that bores through a stubborn blockage. Augering may push blockage through, or it may snag something so you can pull it up and out. If none of these techniques works, see page 72.

DISMANTLING FIXTURE TRAPS

When plunging doesn't clear a clog, or if you've dropped something valuable into a drain, your next step is to dismantle the trap. Before dismantling the trap, see if it has a nutlike clean-out fitting at its lowest point. If so, open it, and fit the auger into the hole. If there is no clean-out, don't be discouraged. Dismantling a trap is not all that difficult or time-consuming. Usually, the worst part of the job is getting a wrench into position if the trap is in an awkward place.

YOU'LL NEED...

TIME: About an hour to dismantle and reassemble a trap.
SKILLS: Beginner plumbing skills.
TOOLS: Tongue-and-groove pliers, Teflon tape or pipe joint compound, some extra washers.

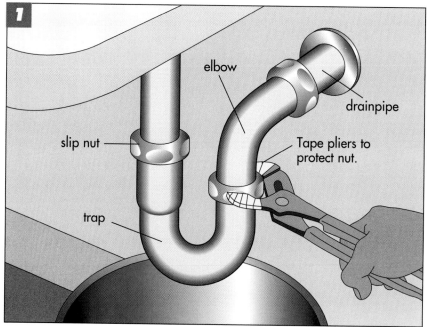

1. Open and drain the trap.

Turn off the faucet firmly. As an extra precaution, turn off the supply valves. Position a bucket to catch the water that will spill out when you remove the trap. Loosen the slip nuts that secure the trap. Protect the nuts from scratches by wrapping electrical tape around the jaws of your wrench or pliers. After a half-turn or so, the nuts can be unscrewed by hand.

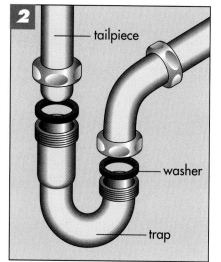

2. Disassemble the trap.

The joints of the trap have a nut and a flexible washer. Keep track of these by pushing them up the tailpiece and elbow. Dump out the water that sits in the trap.

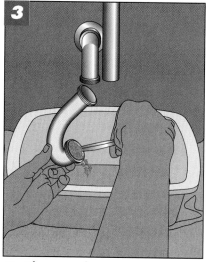

3. Clean out the trap.

Remove any gunk that has collected. Clean the inside of the trap with a small wire brush, or run a piece of cloth through it. Replace any washers that show signs of wear, and slide the trap back into position.

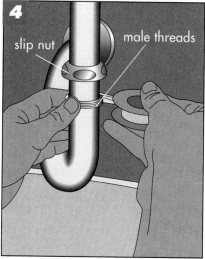

4. Reassemble.

Wrap the male threads with Teflon tape or brush on joint compound. Position trap, slide washers into place, and hand-tighten the slip nuts. Use an adjustable wrench for final tightening. Test for leaks by filling the bowl then removing the plug. Tighten slip nut if necessary.

REPLACING SINK STRAINERS

A slight leak under the sink at the tailpiece is likely the result of a poor seal between the strainer body and the sink. To check for this, plug the sink, fill the bowl, and look for drips. If water drips from where the strainer body joins the sink, disassemble the strainer and apply new putty. Leaks may also occur where the tailpiece joins the strainer body. If so, tighten the slip nut. If that does not solve the problem, replace the washer.

YOU'LL NEED...

TIME: About two hours to disassemble and reassemble a strainer.
SKILLS: Intermediate plumbing techniques.
TOOLS: Adjustable wrench (and possibly a spud wrench), putty knife, plumber's putty, Teflon joint compound. You may need replacement parts.

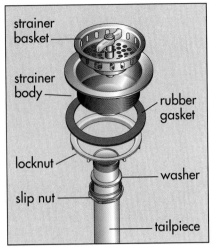

Sink strainer parts
Waste that would clog the drain is captured by the sink strainer. Its wide bowl is held snug against the sink bottom by the locknut. Putty and a rubber gasket sandwich the sink for a tight seal. The next important joint is where the strainer body meets the tailpiece. Here the seal is made watertight with a washer and a slip nut.

1. Remove the tailpiece.
Loosen the slip nut beneath the strainer body and the slip nut above the trap bend using an adjustable wrench. Finish unscrewing it by hand, and remove the tailpiece.

2. Remove the locknut.
Removing the locknut can be difficult, especially if it is hard to get to. Consider purchasing a spud wrench, which is specially designed to fit on locknuts. Otherwise, tap gently with a hammer and screwdriver to loosen the nut.

3. Remove old putty.
Use a putty knife to scrape the old putty from the drain opening. Clean the opening thoroughly with a scouring pad soaked with paint thinner. If you will be reusing the strainer, clean off the flange of the strainer as well.

4. Apply putty, and reinstall.
Make a rope of putty, and place it on the lip of the drain opening. Press the strainer into the opening. From under the sink, slip on the rubber gasket and the friction ring; screw on the locknut. Tighten the locknut until the strainer nests completely into the sink. Reinstall the tailpiece.

AUGERING TECHNIQUES

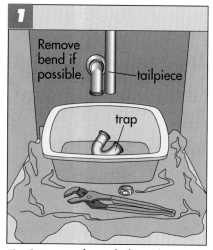

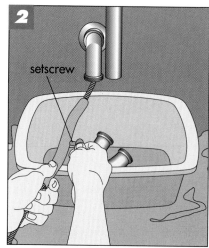

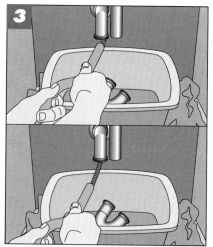

1. Set up a drop cloth and pan.
Be prepared for a mess. Place a drop cloth and a dishpan below the drain opening. Wearing gloves, remove the trap and elbow (see page 72) as well as the pipe leading to the wall. Loosen the setscrew of the auger, and push the auger cable in until you feel it meet resistance.

2. Set the screw, and crank.
Give yourself 6–8 inches of cable to work with, and tighten the setscrew. Crank the auger handle clockwise, and push in until the auger moves forward. Once it is past an obstruction like a bend in the pipe, you may be able to push the cable in without cranking.

3. Push and pull.
Augers can pass through soft obstructions such as soap clogs. Use a push-and-pull motion to ream out such clogs. If the auger comes to a place where it will not crank easily, pull it out. Often the blockage will come out with it. Sometimes you can use the auger to clear the line by pushing the blockage through to a larger pipe.

UNCLOGGING SHOWERS

If a shower stall drains sluggishly, try filling the base with an inch of water and plunging. If the clogged shower drain does not respond to plunging, remove the strainer and attempt to clear the blockage with the two methods shown here. Begin by prying up the strainer with a screwdriver. (Some strainers may have a center screw. Remove it, then pry up.)

YOU'LL NEED...
TIME: Allow yourself two hours to try both methods.
SKILLS: Beginner plumbing skills.
TOOLS: Auger, garden hose attached to a spout, rags.

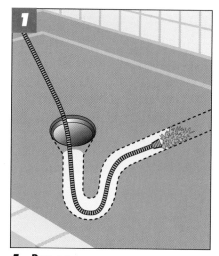

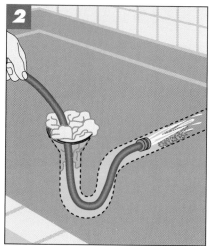

1. Run an auger.
Push an auger down the drain and through the trap. Push and pull to remove a soap clog. If the auger hits a blockage, pull out the auger. The blockage may come with it. If it doesn't, push the auger to try to force the clog into a larger pipe.

2. Push in a hose.
If all else fails, try forcing out the blockage with a hose. Stick it in as far as it will easily go, and pack rags tightly around the hose at the drain opening. Hold everything in place, and have a helper turn the water fully on and off a few times.

UNCLOGGING TUBS

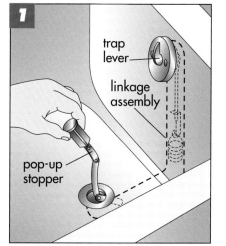

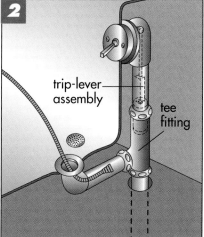

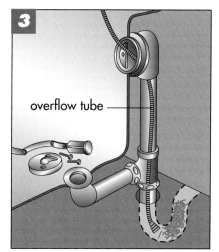

1. Plunge.
Try plunging first. If your tub has a pop-up stopper, remove it before plunging. Wiggle it to free the linkage assembly—the mechanism that connects the trap lever with the stopper mechanism. Before plunging, plug the overflow, and run an inch or so of water in the tub to help the plunger seal.

2. Auger through the strainer.
If plunging doesn't work, thread in an auger. The tub will have a stopper or a trip-lever assembly like the one above. Pry up or unscrew the strainer to insert the auger. This method will reach only to the tee fitting. If the clog is farther down, you'll have to go through the overflow tube.

3. Auger through the overflow.
Remove the pop-up or trip-lever assembly by unscrewing the plate and pulling out the parts (see page 78). Feed the auger down through the overflow tube and into the trap and beyond. If the auger goes in a long way and the stoppage remains, find a clean-out point on the main drain and auger there.

CLEANING DRUM TRAPS

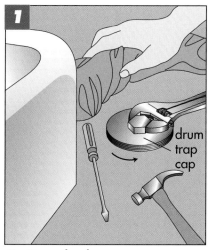

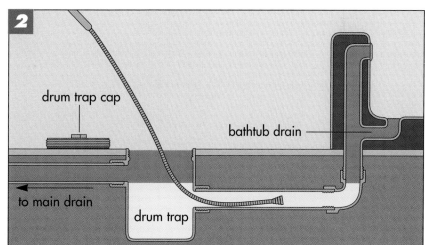

1. Open the drum trap.
Many older bathrooms have a removable metal cap on the floor, usually near the tub. This covers a drum trap. Before opening it, bail out the tub, and remove standing water with rags or a large sponge.

2. Auger through the drum trap.
Removing the cap may be difficult. If a wrench does not do the trick, use a hammer and cold chisel or screwdriver. Damage the trap cap if necessary (it can be replaced easily), but don't hurt the threads on the trap. Open the trap slowly, watching for water to well up

around the threads. If the trap is full, work the auger away from the tub toward the main drain. If the trap is only partially full (as shown), the obstruction is between the tub and the trap, so auger back and forth. Drum traps are no longer to code and should be replaced with a P-trap.

UNCLOGGING TOILETS

When a toilet clogs, do not continue to flush it. Additional flushing will not push objects through and may flood the bathroom floor. Instead, bail out the toilet until the bowl is about half full. More water than this can lead to a sloshy mess while plunging, but too little water will prevent the plunger from making a tight seal around the bowl's outlet. Add water to the toilet if necessary. Most toilet clogs occur because the toilet trap is blocked. If plunging and using a toilet auger do not clear things up, the waste-vent stack may be blocked.

CAUTION!
Never attempt to unclog a toilet with a chemical drain cleaner. Chances are, it won't do the job, and you'll be forced to plunge or auger through a strong solution that could burn your skin or eyes.

EXPERTS' INSIGHT

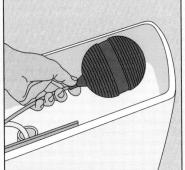

How to stop a toilet overflow
If the toilet begins to overflow, act fast. Remove everything atop the tank, and take off the lid. Pull the float up, and push down on the flapper at the tank bottom. The flush will stop.

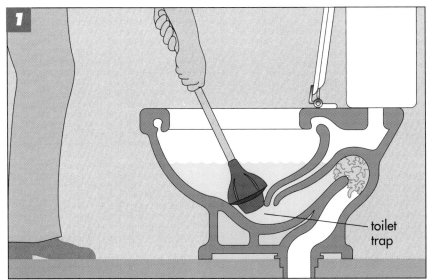

toilet trap

1. Plunge.
An ordinary plunger can clear a toilet, but the molded-cup type shown here generates stronger suction. Work up and down vigorously for about a dozen strokes, then quickly yank away the plunger.

If the water disappears with a glug, it's likely the plunging has succeeded. But don't flush yet. First pour in more water, until the bowl empties several times. If plunging doesn't work, the toilet will have to be augered.

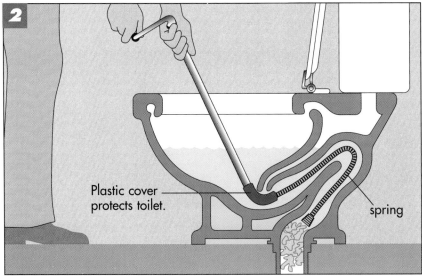

Plastic cover protects toilet.

spring

2. Use a closet auger.
A closet auger makes short work of most toilet stoppages. This specialized tool has a long handle with a plastic cover at the bend to protect your toilet from scratches. To operate it, pull the spring all the way up into the handle so the spring barely protrudes from the plastic protective cover on the end

of the auger. Insert the bit into the bowl outlet, and crank. If you meet resistance, pull back slightly, wiggle the handle, and try again. A closet auger can grab and pull many blockages but not solid objects such as toys. If you hear something other than the auger rattling around, remove the toilet to get at the item (see page 56).

CLEARING MAIN DRAINS AND SEWER LINES

If more than one of your fixtures is sluggish or clogged, or if plunging and augering fail to solve the problem, you may have a clogged drain or sewer line. Look for clean-outs, places where you can remove a large nut and slip in an auger.

Start with the highest clean-out you can find that is below the clogged fixture. If augering it does not work, continue working downward. Sometimes it proves best to go up on the roof and run an auger down through the vent stack. This job often warrants calling in a plumber or a drain-cleaning service, especially if the line is clogged with tree roots.

> **CAUTION!**
> Before removing any clean-out plug from a main drain line, have buckets on hand to catch the wastewater.

Auger a main drain.
Look for a clean-out near the bottom of your home's soil stack. Loosen the plug of the clean-out. If water flows out, the blockage is below. (If no water flows out, the blockage is holding the water above, so replace the clean-out

plug and auger from a higher point.) Insert the auger into the opening, and run it back and forth several times (see page 74). Another solution is to use a blow bag. Once the blow bag is in place, run the water in the hose full force on and off several times.

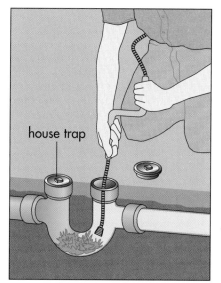

Auger a house trap.
If neither procedure works, move farther down the line. Some houses have a house trap near where the drain line leaves the house. Open one of the two plugs, and thread in an auger. The blockage may be in the trap itself.

Clear a sewer line.
If the blockage still does not go away, the outdoor sewer line may be blocked. Often, fine tree roots work their way into the line, creating a tough blockage that can only be removed with a heavy auger with a cutting bit.

First try feeding in a garden hose to push and flush out the obstruction. If that doesn't work, call in a professional or rent a heavy-duty power auger. Running one of these is a two-person job. Get a demonstration from the rental center on its use.

ADJUSTING DRAIN ASSEMBLIES

If the water in your bathroom sink or tub gradually leaks out when you've stopped the drain, or if it doesn't drain out as quickly as you would like, you may need to adjust your drain assembly.

Before dismantling the assembly, pull up the strainer or stopper, and remove any hair or other debris hanging from it. Next, thoroughly clean away soap or other gunk that may be keeping the strainer or stopper from seating properly.

YOU'LL NEED...
TIME: An hour for most adjustments.
SKILLS: Basic plumbing skills.
TOOLS: Screwdriver, pliers.

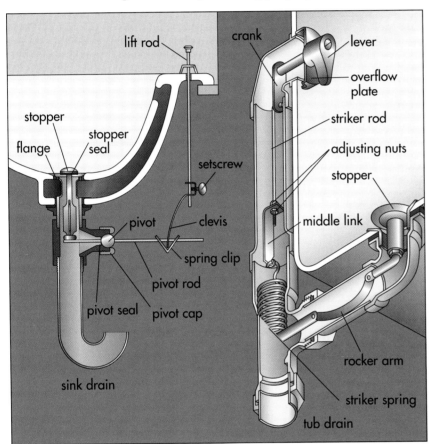

Pop-up drains

If you've cleaned out the strainer and stopper, and the problem persists, check the stopper seal. If it's damaged, replace any rubber parts, or replace the stopper itself. Look for signs of wear on the flange the stopper seats into.

On a bathroom sink, examine the pivot rod. When the stopper is closed, it should slant slightly up from the pivot to the clevis. If it doesn't, loosen the setscrew, raise or lower the clevis on the lift rod, and retighten the screw.

If the stopper doesn't operate as easily now as you would like, squeeze the spring clip, pull the pivot rod out of the clevis, and reinsert it into the next higher or lower hole. If water drips from the pivot, try tightening its cap. If the pivot still drips, you may need to replace the seal inside.

To adjust a tub pop-up, unscrew the overflow plate, withdraw the entire assembly, and loosen the adjusting nuts. If the stopper doesn't seat tightly, move the middle link higher on the striker rod. If the tub is slow to drain, lower the link.

Trip-lever drain

A trip lever lifts and lowers a seal plug at the base of the overflow tube. When the seal plug drops into its seat, water from the tub drain can't get past. But because the plug is hollow, water can still flow through the overflow tube through the overflow passage in the seal plug.

Dismantle and adjust a trip lever as you would a tub pop-up unit. Also, check the seal on the bottom of the plug, and replace it if it appears to be worn.

CLEANING SHOWERHEADS

If your showerhead sprays unevenly, take it apart and clean it, or replace it. If it leaks at the arm, or if it doesn't stay in position, tighten the retainer or collar nut. If that doesn't work, replace the O-ring—or replace the showerhead.

If you want to replace your showerhead, take the old one with you to your supplier to make sure you get one that will fit. You'll find a wide range of styles and features.

YOU'LL NEED...
TIME: About an hour for removal and scrubbing; overnight soaking for a thorough cleaning.
SKILLS: Basic plumbing skills.
TOOLS: Wrench, screwdriver, sharp-pointed tool or thin wire, toothbrush.

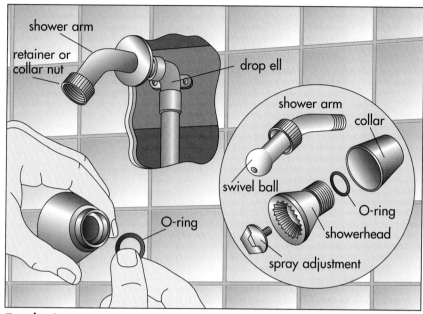

Two basic types
Newer showerheads simply screw onto the shower arm, the chromed pipe that extends from the wall. Older models require a shower arm with a ball-shaped end that acts as a swivel (see inset). In most cases, you can switch to a newer style by replacing the shower arm. If you wish to replace the shower arm, remove it from the drop ell. Wrap Teflon tape around the threads of the new shower arm before screwing it into place.

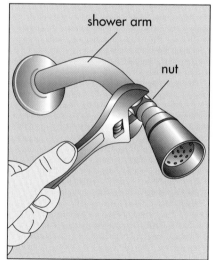

Removing a showerhead
This is a simple matter of unscrewing the nut at the shower arm. Take care not to mar the finish of the shower head or arm: Use a wrench rather than pliers. For an added precaution, cushion your tool with a rag as you work.

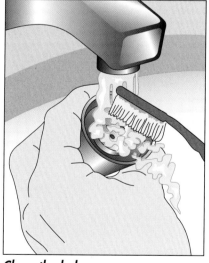

Clean the holes.
Shower heads often spray unevenly because the tiny holes have gotten clogged with mineral deposits. Use an old toothbrush to clean the head. Then run a sharp blast of water backward through the showerhead.

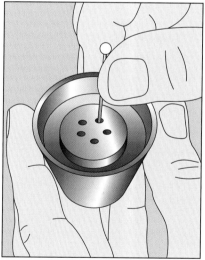

Dismantle and clean.
For a thorough cleaning, take the head apart, use a pin to poke out any mineral buildup or debris, and brush away all deposits. Then soak the parts in vinegar overnight to dissolve remaining mineral deposits. Reassemble and reinstall the showerhead.

PLANNING FOR NEW FIXTURES

Most improvements shown in this book are add-ons, where you simply hook new fittings or fixtures to existing pipes. Running new lines takes coping with the constraints of your situation and an understanding of how supply, drain, and vent pipes work.

New supply lines are the easiest to plan. They require no slope or venting, just the correct pipe size (see box). You can run them wherever you need them.

Far trickier are the drain-waste-vent (DWV) lines that carry away water, waste, and gases. The illustrations below and on page 81 show straightforward ways to tap in for a new fixture. Your situation may not be this simple and may require the skill of a professional.

For any new installation, even a minor one, you'll probably need to apply to your local building department for a permit and arrange with them to have the work inspected before you cover up any new pipes.

MEASUREMENTS

SIZING SUPPLY LINES

Check with your local building department for the supply line size required. As a general rule, most departments require that a line supplying one or two fixtures can be ½ inch. Any line supplying three or more fixtures must be at least ¾ inch.

Planning drain lines

The first step in planning an extension of your plumbing system is to map out exactly where existing lines run. Your home probably has a drainage arrangement similar to the one shown. Notice that some of the fixtures (toilet, double sink) cluster near a wet wall containing the main stack. A wet wall is usually a few inches thicker than other walls to accommodate the 3- or 4-inch-diameter stack that runs up through the roof. (A way to find a wet wall is to note the location of the stack on the roof.)

The fixtures drain directly into the main stack or into horizontal runs that slope downward at a pitch of at least ¼ inch per running foot. Fixtures more than a few feet from the stack (like the bathtub and bathroom sink shown) must be vented with a loop that goes up and back to the stack. Called a revent or a circuit vent, this branch can be concealed inside walls and floors of normal thickness. Fixtures even farther away (like the shower and utility sink shown) may require a separate new stack. Requirements vary on revents and new vents, so check local codes.

Position the new fixtures as close as possible to an existing stack to minimize wall damage.

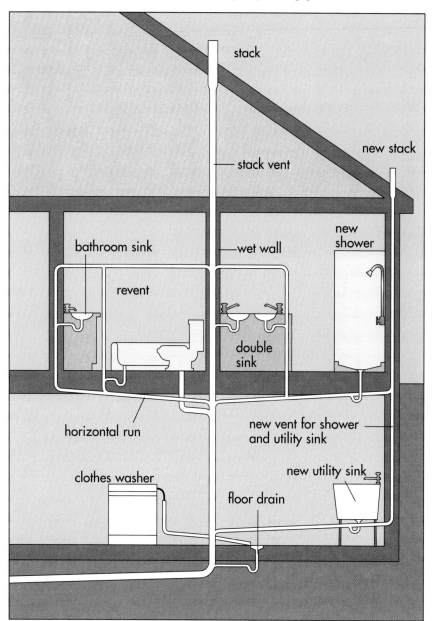

stack

stack vent

new stack

bathroom sink

revent

wet wall

new shower

double sink

horizontal run

new vent for shower and utility sink

new utility sink

clothes washer

floor drain

VENTING POSSIBILITIES

*T*hink of a main stack as a two-way chimney: Water and wastes go down; gases go up. Just as you wouldn't install a fireplace without a chimney, neither should you consider adding a fixture without properly venting it. Strangle the air supply of a drain, and you risk creating a siphoning effect that can suck water out of traps. This in turn breaks the seal that provides protection from gas backup—and often retards the flow of wastes as well.

Codes are specific about how you must vent fixtures. These requirements differ from one locality to another, so check your community's regulations for details about the systems shown here.

With unit venting—sometimes referred to as common venting—two similar fixtures share the same stack fitting. This method allows you to put a new fixture back to back with one that already exists. The fixtures are installed on opposite sides of the wet wall. To install a unit vent, open up the wall, replace the existing sanitary tee with a sanitary cross, and connect both traps to it. The drains of unit-vented fixtures must be at the same height.

Wet venting uses a section of one fixture's drain line to double as the vent for another. Not all codes permit wet venting. Those that do often specify that the vertical drain be at least one pipe size larger than the upper fixture drain. In no case can it be smaller than the lower drain.

Regardless of how you vent a fixture, codes limit the distance between the trap outlet and the vent. These distances depend on the size of the drain line you're running. For 1¼-, 1½-, and 2-inch drain lines—the sizes you'll most likely be working with—2, 3, and 5 feet, respectively, are typical distances. (For help adding plastic drain line see page 86. For how to tap into a cast-iron drain, see page 87.)

Often the best way to install a new fixture is with a revent, or circuit vent. Clear this with your local building department first. They may not allow you to do this with heavy-use items such as toilets or showers.

Sometimes, the only solution is to install a separate vent running up through the roof (see page 88). In some situations—especially if the fixture is on the top floor—it may be relatively simple.

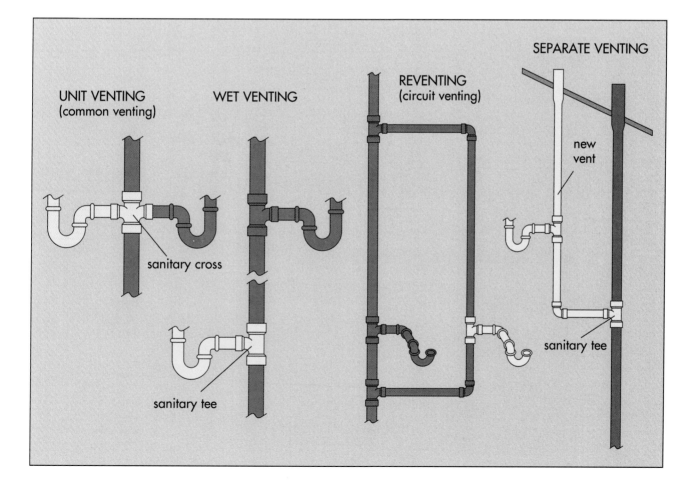

UNIT VENTING (common venting)

WET VENTING

REVENTING (circuit venting)

SEPARATE VENTING

sanitary cross

sanitary tee

new vent

sanitary tee

ROUGHING IN TUBS, SHOWERS, AND TOILETS

Plan the location of your bathroom fixtures carefully: A couple of inches one way or the other can make the difference between a bathroom that is comfortable and one that feels cramped and inconvenient.

Begin by mapping the floor of your bathroom on a piece of graph paper. Cut out small-scale pieces of paper that represent the fixtures. Move the pieces until you find the most usable configuration. If a door opens inward, make sure it can swing completely without hitting a fixture.

The dimensions given in the drawings at right show the minimum requirements for ease of use. Do not place fixtures closer to each other than specified. Once you decide on your floor plan, mark your floors and walls for the rough-in dimensions, using the dimensions shown below right.

EXPERTS' INSIGHT

FINDING DRAINPIPES

■ Before you figure how to rough in your new drains, you need to find the existing drain. Start at the basement or crawl space. If you see a 3- or 4-inch stack, it probably runs straight up through the roof. Or, look for a plumbing access panel. You may have one on the other side of the wall behind your bathroom fixtures. (Often you'll find it in a closet.) Remove the access panel, and peer inside with a flashlight.

■ If you notice a wall is thicker than the standard 4½ inches, chances are it contains drainpipes. Toilets usually are placed near stacks.

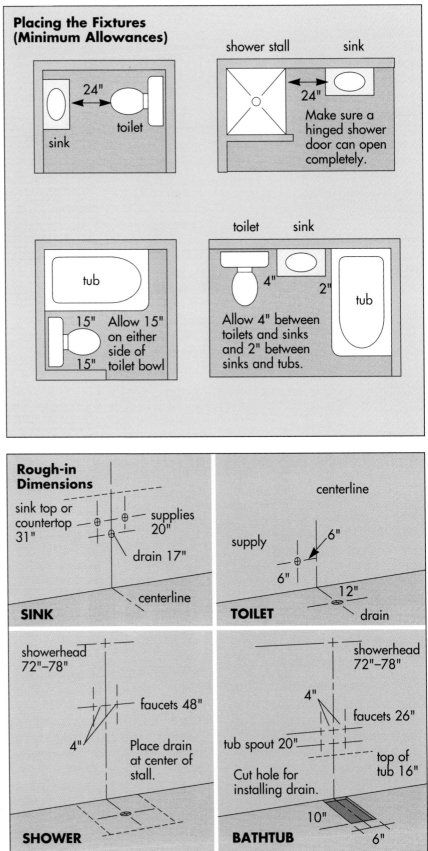

Placing the Fixtures (Minimum Allowances)

sink   toilet   24"

shower stall   sink   24"   Make sure a hinged shower door can open completely.

tub   15"   15"   Allow 15" on either side of toilet bowl

toilet   sink   4"   2"   tub   Allow 4" between toilets and sinks and 2" between sinks and tubs.

Rough-in Dimensions

SINK — sink top or countertop 31"   supplies 20"   drain 17"   centerline

TOILET — centerline   6"   6"   12"   supply   drain

SHOWER — showerhead 72"–78"   faucets 48"   4"   Place drain at center of stall.

BATHTUB — showerhead 72"–78"   4"   faucets 26"   tub spout 20"   Cut hole for installing drain.   top of tub 16"   10"   6"

Once you've finished planning, cut holes in your walls and floors for installing drain lines and supply stubs, the supply lines that stick out a bit from the wall and are ready to accept stop valves.

Patching walls and floors can be more time-consuming than the plumbing itself. Where possible, limit your cuts to areas that will be covered by the fixtures. Cut drywall or plaster neatly so it can be patched easily. Don't forget to install venting (see pages 80–81).

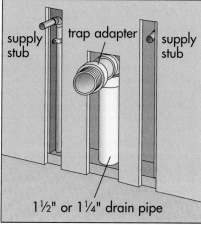

Rough-in a sink.
If you are installing a vanity cabinet, you have latitude for placing the drain and supply stubs. For a wall-hung sink or a pedestal sink, hold the fixture up against the wall, and mark the best locations for drain and supply stubs (see pages 90–93). In most cases, it is best to position the supply stubs within 12 inches of the faucet.

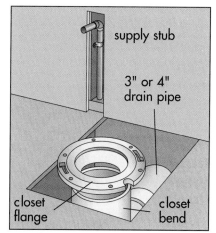

Rough-in a toilet.
Be careful to place the closet bend the correct distance from the wall—usually 12 inches to the center of the drain. (Double-check the requirements for your toilet.) A closet flange will sit on top of the floor after you have patched and surfaced it. Only a cold water supply stub is needed. Place it where it will be unnoticeable.

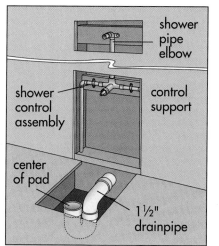

Rough-in a shower only.
To correctly position the drain, set the base in place and measure from the walls. Allow for wall surfacing (see pages 94–95). To spare patching later, cut the floor so the base will cover the hole. Install a P-trap below the level of the floor at the level required by the drain assembly kit. Install the control assembly. Its size determines how far apart the supply pipes should be. Firmly attach the shower pipe to framing.

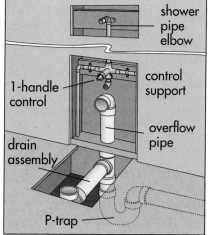

Rough-in a tub and shower.
Cut the floor so the tub will cover the hole. Install a P-trap and bathtub drain assembly. It will be somewhat unstable until you connect it to the tub. The one-handle control shown requires that supplies be plumbed horizontally into it. Attach the control and the top of the shower pipe firmly to framing; you will probably need to frame in a piece of lumber between the studs.

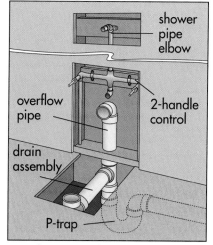

Rough-in a two-handle control.
A two-handle control is easier to install. Set the hot and cold pipes at the same height. Attach the control and the top of the shower pipe elbow to frame supports.

CAUTION!
DON'T WEAKEN JOISTS
Deep notches greatly reduce the strength of joists. Drill holes if possible, or reinforce joists after notching.

TAPPING INTO EXISTING LINES

When you add a sink close to or on the other side of a wet wall—the wall containing working plumbing lines—tie into existing copper supplies and plastic drain lines. (For tapping into cast-iron, see page 87.) If you have trouble locating your drain line in the wall, see the tips on page 82.

Tapping into a wet wall is much less trouble than installing new drain, vent, and supply lines, but it is still a major project. Don't spoil the job by getting one important detail wrong: A telltale sign of an unprofessional plumbing job is when the hot and cold end up on the wrong sides of the sink. People notice if the two are switched. Plan so the hot handle is on the left.

YOU'LL NEED...
TIME: About a day.
SKILLS: Joining copper or plastic pipe, basic carpentry skills.
TOOLS: Keyhole saw, utility knife, tubing cutter, fine-toothed saw, miter box, tongue-and-groove pliers, hacksaw or reciprocating saw, ratchet with socket, torch.

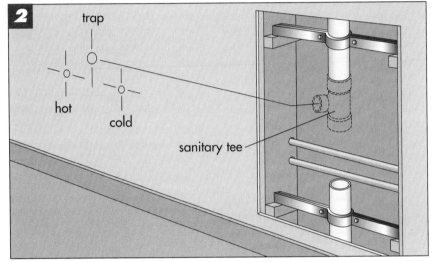

1. Anchor the drain line.
NOTE: *Shut off the water, and drain the lines.* Open up the wet wall to the center of the studs on either side, so you will have a nailing surface for patching later. You may have to make a separate hole for access to the supply pipes. Anchor the stack by attaching riser clamps above and below the area you will cut.

2. Lay out the installation.
Plan out the fixture's rough-in dimensions (see pages 82–83), and mark them on the wall. Be sure the location doesn't exceed the maximum distance permitted by local codes. To determine the point at which the fixture will tie into the stack, draw a line that slopes from the center of the drain trap at ¼ inch per foot. Being careful to cut squarely, use a hacksaw or reciprocating saw to remove a section of stack 8 inches longer than the sanitary tee you'll be installing.

CAUTION!
AVOID DISASTER
Tell family members not to use any toilets positioned above the place where you have cut the stack, or you will receive an extremely rude surprise. Also, be aware that sewer gases can escape from an opened stack. Cap the lines with duct tape, or stuff rags in them if they will be left open for more than a few minutes.

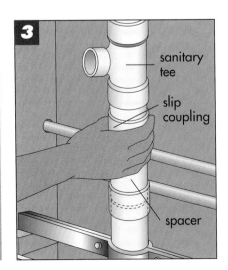

3. Install the sanitary tee.
In most cases, the sanitary tee should be sized to accept 1½-inch pipe; for bathroom sinks, 1¼-inch is sometimes acceptable. Fit the tee, two spacers, and two slip couplings into place as shown. Slide the couplings up and down to secure the spacers. Just dry-fit the pieces at this point; don't cement them until the rest of the run is completed.

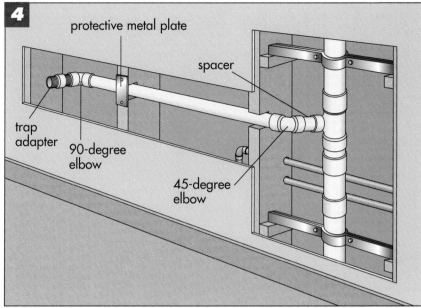

4. Install the drainpipe.
Cut out a strip of drywall, and notch the studs just deep enough to support the pipes. In most cases, it works best to use a 45-degree elbow and a short spacer at the stack, and a 90-degree elbow and a trap adapter at the trap. Once you're sure the pipe slopes at ¼ inch per foot, scribe all the pieces with alignment marks, disassemble, prime, and cement the drainpipe pieces together (see page 27).

EXPERTS' INSIGHT

DON'T OVERNOTCH
Although the situation is not as critical as with floor joists (see page 83), it is important not to weaken wall studs by cutting deep notches in them. Notch only as much as you need.

PROTECT PIPES FROM NAIL PUNCTURES
To eliminate any possibility of poking a hole in a pipe when you nail the drywall back on, protect drainpipes with metal plates placed over notches. If you can, run supply pipes through holes drilled in the center of studs.

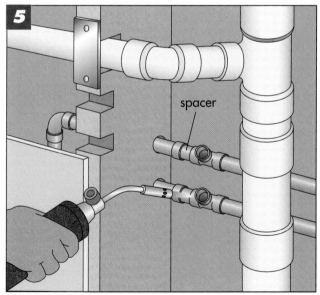

5. Install supply tees.
Tap into copper or plastic supply lines using spacers, slip couplings, and tees similar to those you used on the drainpipe. (For soldering in copper joints, see pages 18–20.) If you tap into galvanized steel supply lines, you may have to cut and remove sections of pipe and install unions. Be sure to use a transition fitting if you're mixing pipe materials (see page 14).

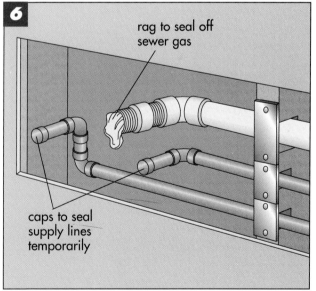

6. Run and cap supply lines.
Run pipes over to the fixture location using 90-degree elbows and pipe as needed. Use 90-degree elbows and short pieces to bring the lines past the wall surface. Stuff a rag in the drain to seal off sewer gas. Solder caps on the ends of the supply lines, turn on the water, and test for leaks. Close up the wall, add stop valves (see page 30), and you're ready to install the fixture.

ADDING PLASTIC DRAIN LINES

Cutting, moving, and refitting plastic pipe are all simple jobs—as long as you have a plastic waste stack and easy access to the drainpipe.

Don't forget that every drain line must be properly vented (see pages 80–81). Be sure you have this planned before you start cutting into the drainpipe. You may need to tap in at a second, higher point for the vent.

YOU'LL NEED...

TIME: If you have easy access to the existing drain, assume a half day for this assembly.
SKILLS: Cutting pipe straight, measuring, aligning, and cementing plastic pipe.
TOOLS: Hacksaw or fine-toothed saw, marker, utility knife, drill with holesaw bit or a reciprocating saw.

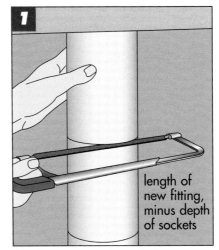

length of new fitting, minus depth of sockets

1. Cut out a section of pipe.
Measure the new sanitary tee to see how much of the old pipe you need to remove. Take into account the depth of the sockets (see pages 16–17). Be sure that both sides of the existing pipe are supported, so they'll stay in position after the cut is made. Cut with a hacksaw or fine-toothed saw, and remove any burrs with a utility knife.

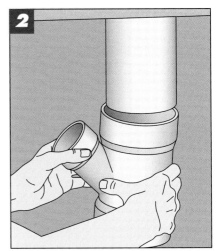

2. Dry-fit the sanitary tee.
First install the top end, then the bottom. You may have to loosen one of your support straps somewhere to give yourself enough play in the pipes to do this. Once the sanitary tee is dry-fit in the desired position, make an alignment mark with a marker.

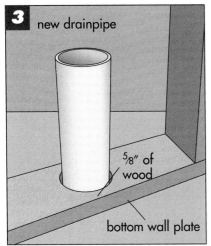

new drainpipe

⅝" of wood

bottom wall plate

3. Cut hole, and install new pipe.
Run pipes to the location of the new fixture (see pages 82–83). If you need to run the drainpipe through wall plates or framing, cut holes to accommodate the pipe. Leave at least ⅝ inch of wood on any side that will receive drywall. This way, nails or screws driven through drywall and into the plate won't pierce the pipe.

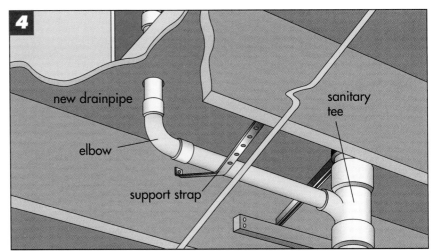

new drainpipe

sanitary tee

elbow

support strap

4. Connect the pieces between.
Connect the new drainpipe to the sanitary tee with elbows and lengths of pipe. Dry-fit the pieces, draw alignment lines, disassemble, prime, and cement the pieces together (see pages 26–27). Support the run with at least one strap for the horizontal run.

CAUTION!
PROTECT YOUR EYES
This is a job in which plenty of dirt, burrs, and sawdust will fall from above. Wear goggles when working above your head.

TAPPING INTO CAST-IRON DRAIN LINES

Cast-iron pipe is used in many older homes for the drain-waste-vent system. Often, one or two large stacks are made of cast-iron, and the lines leading into them are galvanized steel.

Cast-iron is difficult to work with (see the Caution! below). Fortunately, it is no longer required for new installations. However, you may need to run a new drain into an existing cast-iron stack. Most likely, you will have to tap in at two places, one for the drain and one for the vent.

This page shows how to break into a cast-iron stack to replace a cast-iron Y-fitting with a plastic sanitary tee. The same techniques can be used to install a sanitary tee, as shown on page 86.

YOU'LL NEED...

TIME: Set aside a full day, so you can take your time on this difficult project.
SKILLS: Joining plastic pipe and basic carpentry skills.
TOOLS: Cast-iron pipe cutter (rent this tool), socket and ratchet, screwdriver, hacksaw or fine-toothed saw.

CAUTION!
CONSIDER HIRING A PRO
Working with cast-iron is not only difficult, but it is dangerous as well. Cast-iron is heavy, can shatter, and has sharp edges. This is a project that you may want to leave to a professional. Some plumbers may be willing to make the cast-iron connections only, allowing you to save money by making the plastic connections yourself.

1. Support the stack.
Begin by securely supporting the stack from above and making sure that it is well-supported below. (You do not need to move either portion of the cast-iron pipe in order to make the connection.) Use riser clamps specially made for support.

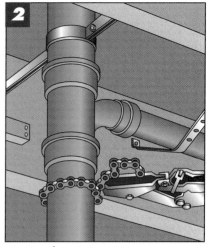

2. Cut the pipe.
Rent a chain-type pipe cutter. Wrap the chain around the stack, hook it, and, with the handles open, crank the chain tight with the turn screw. Draw the handles together. This part of the job takes muscle, but if you follow the manufacturer's directions, you will get a clean cut.

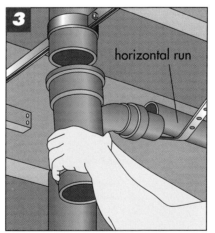

3. Finish cutting, remove fitting.
If you are removing a fitting, make a second cut about 4 inches below the first cut, and cut the horizontal run. If the horizontal pipe is galvanized steel, cut it with a hacksaw. Remove the 4-inch section, and pull the fitting out.

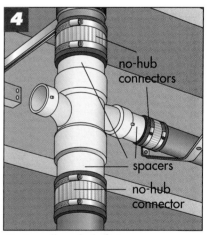

4. Install no-hub fittings.
Install new plastic fittings with no-hub connectors. You may have to use short sections of pipe as spacers. To assemble a no-hub connector, slip the connector over the end of the old pipe, insert the sanitary tee with spacers in place, slide the connector so it bridges the old pipe and the spacers, and install clamps. Tighten clamps with a screwdriver.

ADDING NEW VENTS

If your new fixture is far away from an existing stack, codes may require a new vent. Though it will have to run all the way up through the roof, it may be easier to install than tying into the existing stack. Adding a new stack can be less work than cutting into a wall for a revent and patching afterward, especially if your wall has no insulation and no fire blocking. If you have attic space with exposed pipes, consider running the new vent straight up through the attic. You can tie into the existing vent there.

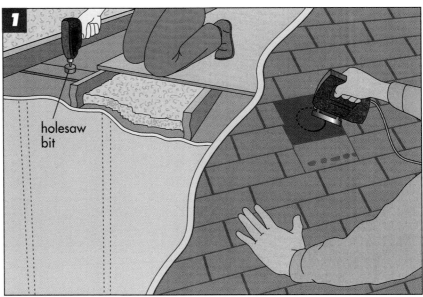

1. Cut holes in the attic, roof.
In the attic, find the top plate of the wall where the new vent is needed. Choose a spot between two studs, and drill down through the plate. Size the hole just big enough to handle the outside diameter of the pipe. (Codes will probably call for a 1½- or 1¼-inch vent.) Mark the point directly above the hole, and drive a nail up through the roof. Remove a shingle; cut a hole with a jigsaw or reciprocating saw. (You may need to cut a larger hole if you're increasing pipe size. See Step 3.) If a rafter is in the way, offset the vent with 45-degree elbows.

2. Install the pipe.
With a helper, slide a pipe through the holes. It usually works best to start at the attic and push down. After everything is dry-fit, prime and cement the joints. Allow more than enough pipe above the roof— you can trim it once the cement has set and you have checked the fit of the flashing.

3. Install roof flashing.
Secure the vent with a riser clamp (see page 84) in the attic. In cold climates, codes call for an increased pipe size where the pipe pierces the roof to prevent freeze-ups from clogging the vent. Slip the flashing over the vent; tuck it under the shingles uphill from the vent. Seal with roofing cement.

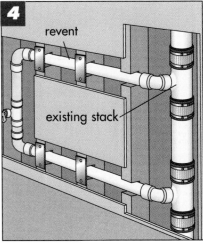

4. Reventing.
If you are close enough to an existing stack, it is often easiest to revent. However, as the illustration shows, this usually means lots of patching afterward. If you will be tying into an old cast-iron stack, you will have to go through all the hassle described on page 87.

RUNNING THE SUPPLY LINES

Once the DWV system is installed, it's time for the easier job of extending supply lines to the new location. If you are tying into old galvanized pipe, look for a convenient union, open it, and dismantle back to the nearest fittings. Otherwise, tee in the supply by cutting a supply pipe and removing both ends (see page 84). Now you are ready to connect new to old. **NOTE:** *Turn the water off, and drain the lines before cutting pipe or opening unions.*

YOU'LL NEED...

TIME: About four hours to tap into two lines and run eight pieces of pipe including fittings.
SKILLS: Measuring, cutting, and soldering copper pipe.
TOOLS: Hacksaw or tubing cutter, propane torch, tongue-and-groove pliers, Crescent wrench.

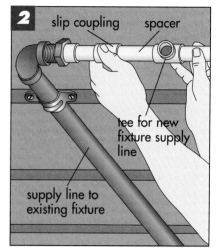

1. dielectric adapter for going from galvanized to copper

1. Tap in with an adapter.

To go from galvanized to copper or plastic (check to be sure your locality permits the use of plastic supplies if you choose this option), use a dielectric adapter like the one shown here. Never hook copper pipe directly to galvanized, or electrolytic action will corrode the connection.

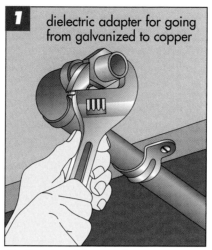

2. slip coupling   spacer
tee for new fixture supply line
supply line to existing fixture

2. Make new pipe connections.

Replace the run you've just removed with copper or plastic pipe and a tee fitting. Splice with a slip coupling and spacer. Solder or cement the pipes and fittings. As you install the pipes leading to the new service, slope the lines slightly so the system can be drained easily.

EXPERTS' INSIGHT

MAINTAINING PRESSURE WHEN ADDING LINES

■ For pipes supplying more than two fixtures, use ¾-inch rather than ½-inch pipe.
■ If you have a long run (more than 25 feet), use ¾-inch pipe. Usually it is best to run ¾-inch pipe into a bathroom, then ½-inch pipe to each fixture.
■ Don't move up from ½-inch to ¾-inch pipe in a line. Step down in dimension, never up.
■ If you have more than four right-angle bends, make some gradual by using 45-degree elbows. Too many sharp turns will reduce water pressure.

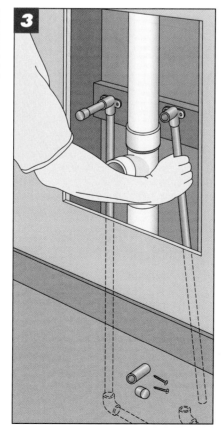

3.

3. Add on drop ells.

At the new fixture, use drop ells instead of regular elbows. Attach them with screws to a piece of wood that is firmly anchored to the framing. Make sure they are positioned 6 to 8 inches apart.

Follow the directions given on pages 18–20 for soldering copper pipes, or see pages 26–27 for cementing plastic pipe. Before soldering copper, open every faucet on the run. Otherwise, heat from the torch can burn out washers and other parts, and built-up steam can rupture a fitting or pipe wall.

Cap the lines, turn on the water, and check for leaks. Don't cover the opening yet; the inspector will probably want to look at the pipes before you patch the wall.

INSTALLING RIMMED SINKS

Setting a new sink in place is one of the truly satisfying plumbing tasks. It signals completion of a fairly easy job that gets noticed by your family.

When shopping for a new deck-mounted fixture, you'll find plenty of options—stainless steel, cast-iron, plastic composite, vitreous china, and more. Nowadays most sinks—for the kitchen and bathroom—are self-rimming, which means you just put some putty on the rim and clamp the sink down on the countertop.

To remove an old sink, first turn off the supply stops or shut off the water to your house and drain the lines. Disconnect the supply lines and the trap joining the sink to the drainpipe. Remove any mounting clips from underneath, and pry the sink up.

YOU'LL NEED...

TIME: Half a day to cut a hole in the vanity top, install the sink, and hook up faucet and drain.
SKILLS: Basic plumbing and carpentry skills.
TOOLS: Sabersaw and extra blades, screwdriver, tongue-and-groove pliers.

1. To install a bathroom sink, first cut an opening.

If you need to cut a hole for the sink, trace the template provided with the sink. Drill an entry hole, and cut using a sabersaw and fine-toothed blade.

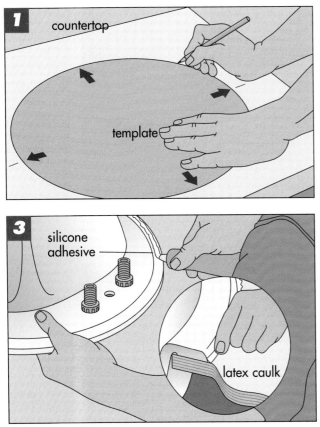

3. Set the sink.

Apply a thick bead of silicone adhesive around the underside of the fixture's flange, about 1/4 inch from the edge. Turn the sink right side up, and lower it carefully into the opening. Press down on the sink; some of the caulk will ooze out. Wipe away the excess with a damp cloth. After the silicone adhesive has set (about two hours), apply latex caulk around the sink.

2. Attach faucet and drain.

Before lowering the sink into the opening, hook up the faucet (see pages 50–51) and drain assembly (see page 78). With bathroom sinks, the drain assembly consists of a basin outlet flange, a drain body, a gasket, a locknut, and a tailpiece, which slides into the P-trap. (Installing these after you install the sink is not only difficult, but you also run a greater risk of damaging the parts.) Lay a bead of plumber's putty around the basin outlet, insert the flange, and screw together the other parts of the drain assembly.

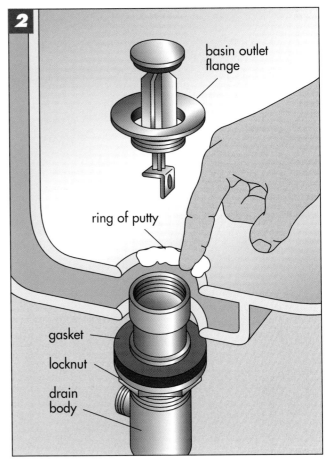

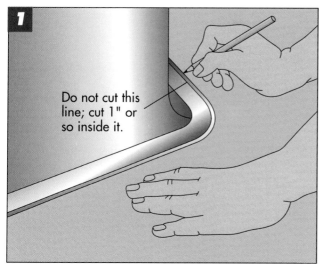

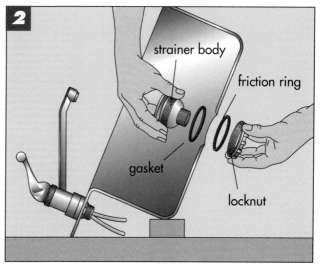

1. For a stainless-steel sink, mark and cut opening.

Turn your sink upside down on the countertop. Make sure it is in the correct position, safely set back from the cabinet beneath. Trace the outline of the sink, then draw a line that is an inch or so to the inside of that outline. Erase the first line to make sure you do not cut it. Test to make sure the sink fits. Cut the opening using a circular saw with a fine-toothed blade for the straight cuts and a sabersaw for curves. Take your time to avoid splintering the laminate.

2. Attach the faucet and strainers.

Attach a basket strainer to each bowl. Lay a bead of putty around the outlet, set the gasket in place, and lower the strainer body into the hole. With your other hand, from underneath, slip the friction ring in place, and screw on the locknut. Tighten, and clean away the putty that oozes out. You also can attach the tailpiece and trap assembly at this point. To install the faucet, see pages 50–51.

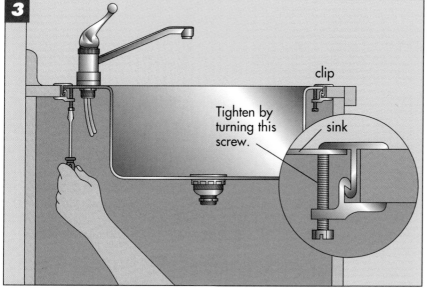

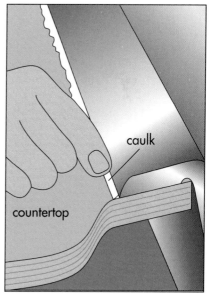

3. Set and secure the sink.

To set the sink, place a rope of plumber's putty all around the rim so it will seal everywhere. Turn the sink right side up, and lower it into the opening. Secure the sink to the countertop with sink clips every 6 to 8 inches. Working from underneath the sink, tighten the clips with a screwdriver. Remove excess putty with a putty knife and a rag dipped in paint thinner.

Install a cast-iron sink.

To set a cast-iron kitchen sink, use the same technique as for the rimmed sink (see page 90). Run a bead of silicone sealant under the rim, turn the sink right side up, set it in place, and wipe away the excess sealant. Run caulk along the edge, and smooth it with a finger.

INSTALLING WALL-HUNG SINKS

Wall-hung bathroom sinks are not as popular as they once were but remain useful where space is limited or a retro style is called for. Installing the bracket support is the most time-consuming part of this job.

YOU'LL NEED...

TIME: A half day to add framing and install a new sink.
SKILLS: Basic plumbing and carpentry skills.
TOOLS: Keyhole saw, hammer, level, screwdriver, tongue-and-groove pliers or pipe wrench.

CAUTION!

WATCH YOUR WEIGHT!
Bracket-supported sinks stand up well to normal everyday use, but warn members of the household not to sit on them. They could crack or pull away from the wall.

Notch studs and anchor a piece of 2×10.

1. Rough-in, provide bracing.
Note: *Be sure to shut off the water, and drain the line.* To remove an old fixture, disconnect the drain and supply lines, and look underneath to see if it is held in by bolts. If so, loosen or cut the bolts. Pull straight up on the sink to dislodge it.

For a new installation, run new supply lines (see pages 84–89), and provide solid framing for the hanger bracket.

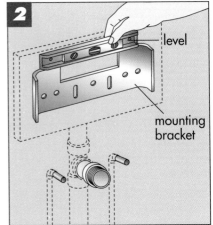

level

mounting bracket

2. Finish wall, anchor bracket.
Install the drywall. You may even want to tape and paint it—it will be easier to do now than after the sink is in place. Secure the hanger bracket to the 2×10 blocking. Use plenty of screws, and make sure the bracket is level. If they are not already in place, equip each supply line with a stop valve (see pages 30–31).

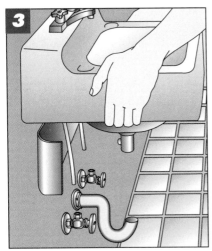

3. Set sink in place.
Turn the sink on its side, and install the faucet and the drain assembly (see pages 50–51, 72). Attach flexible supply lines to the sink. Place the sink above the bracket, press it flat against the wall, and lower it onto the bracket. A flange fits into a corresponding slot in the sink.

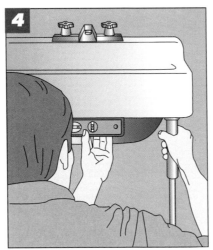

4. Attach legs.
If your sink comes with support legs, insert them into the holes in the bottom of the sink, plumb them, and adjust them so they firmly support the sink. To do this, twist the top portion of each leg. Check to see that the sink is level.

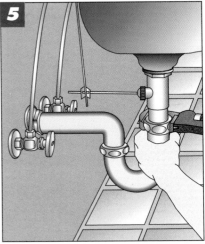

5. Hook up supplies, drain.
Connect the flexible supply lines to the stop valves. Connect the trap to the sink drain and to the drainpipe. Restore water pressure, and check supply lines for leaks. To test the drain for leaks, pull the stopper lever up, fill the bowl, and open the stopper.

INSTALLING PEDESTAL SINKS

Pedestal sinks are popular because of their sleek good looks. They hide the plumbing without a cabinet. However, installation is more difficult than for a regular wall-hung sink or a vanity. You have to get all the plumbing to fit inside the pedestal, and you must attach the sink at the right height so the pedestal fits just beneath it. Watch out for less expensive units that have narrower than usual pedestals.

You'll Need...

TIME: A day to move the plumbing and install the sink.
SKILLS: Basic plumbing and carpentry skills.
TOOLS Keyhole saw, hammer or drill, screwdriver, tongue-and-groove pliers.

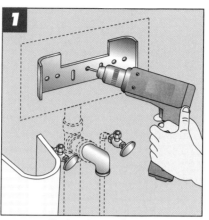

1. Install plumbing, framing.
Note: *Shut off the water.* Open the wall, and install a 2×10 (see page 92). Measure the width of the pedestal, and install the drain and supply lines so they will fit inside it. Finish the walls, and install stop valves. Position the sink and pedestal against the wall to mark the bracket's location. Attach the bracket to the wall.

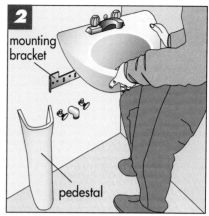

2. Assemble, install the sink.
Carefully set the sink into the bracket, and fasten with the nuts and bolts or toggle bolts provided. Slide the pedestal in, and caulk around the bottom with bathtub caulk. Restore water pressure, and check for leaks.

ADDING VANITIES

Vanities are popular because they add much-needed storage in otherwise wasted space. They're easier to install than a wall-hung or pedestal unit because the sink sits on the vanity rather than hanging from the wall. As a result, measurements and cuts don't have to be as exact. Even finishing the wall is simplified. If your vanity has a back panel, you don't have to finish the wall around the plumbing—the vanity covers it.
Note: *Be sure to shut off the water, and drain the line.*

You'll Need...

TIME: A day to add the vanity and install the basic plumbing.
SKILLS: Basic plumbing and carpentry skills.
TOOLS Sabersaw, screwdriver, channel-type pliers, caulk gun.

1. Install plumbing, cabinet.
Install the supply lines and drain line—be sure they will be covered by the cabinet and won't interfere with the sink. If the cabinet has a back, measure carefully, and cut out holes. Slide the cabinet into position, and level it from side to side and front to back with shims. Anchor it to the wall by driving screws through the cabinet frame and into studs.

2. Hook up the sink top.
Turn the sink top on its side, and install the faucet, the flexible supply lines, and the drain assembly. Run a bead of silicone caulk under the sink to anchor it to the cabinet. Set it on top of the cabinet, and make the final connections. Restore water pressure, and check for leaks.

INSTALLING SHOWERS

A successful shower installation requires careful planning and plenty of work. In most cases, you will need to do three kinds of tasks: framing walls, installing the plumbing, and finishing walls. For information about framing, finishing, and tiling shower stall walls for the projects on this page and page 95, look for books at your local library.

First decide where you would like to put the shower. You need a space at least 32 inches square—36 inches makes for a more comfortable shower—not including the thickness of any new walls you may have to build. Be sure to leave room for the shower door to open and close. See pages 80–81 for help in planning.

Next, plan the rough plumbing. The most important planning issue is how the unit will be vented (see pages 82–83 for options). Make sure the drain line can be installed without seriously weakening your joists. The supply lines are usually easy to plan for—you simply tap into and extend existing lines (see page 85).

Sometimes during new house construction, plumbers install plumbing lines for possible future use. You may be lucky enough to already have the drain line you need poking up through the basement floor.

The final step in planning a shower is choosing the material the shower is made from. There are several kinds: one-, two-, or three-piece prefabricated fiberglass stalls. In addition, you can purchase knockdown units with a base and walls that you put together, freestanding metal units that require no framing, and plastic or concrete shower bases with tiled walls.

A large variety of glass doors are available, or you can simply hang a shower curtain.

EXPERTS' INSIGHT

TIPS FOR PLANNING A NEW SHOWER

■ For a coordinated look, choose the whole ensemble at once: door, stall or tile, base, and faucet and showerhead.

■ Unless you have better than average ventilation or live in an extra-dry area, install a bathroom vent fan near the shower. The shower will introduce a great deal of moisture that could damage walls and lead to mildew problems if it is not properly vented.

■ Consider hiring a professional to install the shower base with drain and vent. Installing the showerhead and controls and finishing the walls are comparatively easy tasks.

■ Although 32-inch bases and prefab units are available, most adults will feel cramped in them. If at all possible, install a 36-inch base.

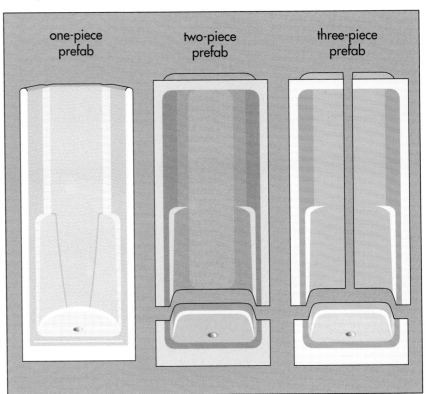

Three types of prefab shower stalls Prefabricated stalls usually include the base and come with framing instructions. A freestanding one-piece unit is the easiest to install, but may be too bulky to haul into your bathroom. When logistics require, use a multipiece unit.

Other options include a free-standing metal unit, usually installed in basements as utility showers. Or you may choose to construct tiled walls around a shower base (see page 95). Tile also offers wide color options.

INSTALLING PREFAB UNITS

Purchase the unit before you build the framing, and consult the manufacturer's instructions, closely regarding the exact dimensions needed. You may need to leave one wall of framing open until the unit is in place.

Install the drain in the center of the stall, following manufacturer's instructions. Frame for the unit, providing a nailing surface where needed. Check framing for plumb.

YOU'LL NEED...

TIME: Several days in most situations.
SKILLS: Good plumbing, carpentry, and wall-preparation and finishing skills.
TOOLS: A complete set of plumbing and carpentry tools (a reciprocating saw often comes in handy).

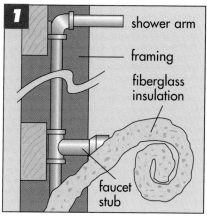

1. Anchor plumbing.
Anchor supply lines, the faucet, and the shower arm to framing—don't rely on the unit's walls for support. (See pages 82–83.)

To reduce noise, install insulation between the studs. Slice the insulation's foil or paper face so moisture will not get trapped between the insulation and the walls of the prefab shower.

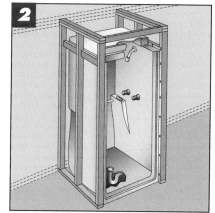

2. Attach unit, finish walls.
Drill holes in the unit's walls for the faucet and shower arm. Slide the parts into place, and attach to the framing. Install the finish plumbing pieces: drain piece, shower handle, escutcheon, and showerhead. Caulk the seams, and check for leaks. Finish the walls, and install a shower door.

PREPARING FOR TILE

Install the drain and the shower base, and check for leaks by pouring water down the drain. Install any necessary new framing. Be sure to leave an opening that's the right size for your shower door. Purchase the door kit in advance so you can check the finished opening dimensions. Make sure new and old walls are plumb, or you'll end up with crooked grout lines. Install the shower supply lines, faucet, and shower arm before preparing the walls for tile.

YOU'LL NEED...

TIME: Two days, once the plumbing is in place.
SKILLS: Carpentry and tiling.
TOOLS: Knife, drill, taping knife, notched trowel, grout float.

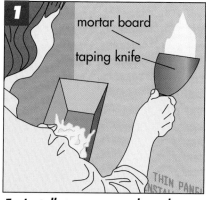

1. Install, tape cement board.
Check for plumb and any waviness in the walls. Shim the walls as required. Use cement board for the most stable and long-lasting subsurface. Cut this material with a utility knife in the same way as drywall, and attach it with galvanized screws. Cover the screws or nails and the corner joints with wallboard compound using a taping knife.

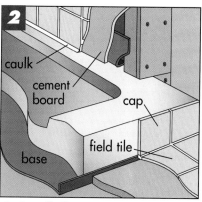

2. Install tile.
Plan your tile job carefully. Use field tiles for most of the walls, but at all exposed edges, use caps. These have one finished edge. Special corner pieces have two finished edges. Apply the adhesive with a notched trowel, set the tiles, and let them dry for 24 hours. Apply grout with a grout float, wipe away excess, and clean it several times. Apply bathroom caulk to all inside corners.

INSTALLING HAND SHOWERS

A hand shower attached to an existing shower is a luxurious addition to a shower/tub area. A hand shower attached to a tub faucet can be an economical alternative to a complete shower installation, giving you a shower without the trouble of cutting open walls and installing new plumbing. Whichever type of unit you choose, a variety of showerheads are available, ranging from the simple to the exotic. Installing them is quick and easy, a straightforward bathroom upgrade well within the skill level of any do-it-yourselfer.

YOU'LL NEED...

TIME: An hour or two for either installation.
SKILLS: No special skills needed.
TOOLS: Screwdriver, tongue-and-groove pliers, drill, hammer, awl.

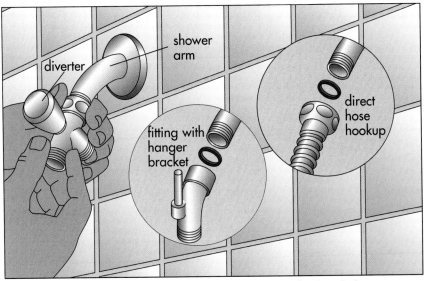

At an existing shower

Remove the showerhead. Protect chrome parts from scratches by taping the jaws of the pliers. Clean the threads. If your shower arm does not have male threads, replace it with one that does. Wrap the threads with Teflon tape, and screw on the hand shower with pliers. The hand shower connector may have a diverter (which allows you to choose either the fixed or the hand-held head), a hanger bracket (the new head fits on it), or a direct hose hookup (the hose attaches to the shower arm). For the latter, install a shower hanger (see below).

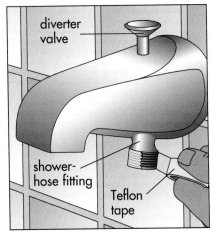

A tub-only unit

Remove the old spout by inserting the handle of a hammer into the spout opening and turning counterclockwise. Clean the pipe threads to which the spout was attached. You may need to remove the existing nipple and install one that is longer or shorter. Apply Teflon tape, and screw on the new spout with diverter valve. Attach the hose to the shower-hose fitting.

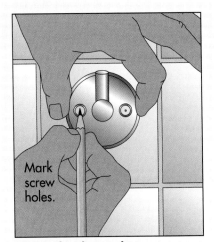

Mount the shower hanger.

Some hangers can be mounted by simply peeling the paper off the backs and sticking them in place. Be sure the wall is absolutely clean and dry before doing so. For a more permanent solution, hold the hanger in position, and mark for the screw holes. With a hammer and a

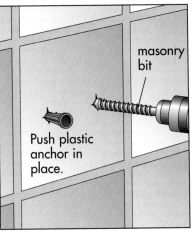

sharp-pointed awl or nail, tap a little nick in the tile—gently, so you don't crack the tile. This will keep your masonry bit from slipping on the ceramic glaze as you start the hole. Drill the holes, push plastic anchors in place, and secure the hanger with screws.

INSTALLING WATER FILTRATION SYSTEMS

If you receive municipal water, information concerning water quality should be available at city hall. However, if you have a well, you are on your own. Your local department of health can recommend a company to test your water to see if you need a filter. A test for bacteria is relatively inexpensive, but a full test that includes a search for pesticides, organic matter, and other potential problems can be costly. Local officials should be able to tell you if other people in your area have had similar tests done and what, if any, contaminants were found.

If the taste of your drinking water is your major concern, try a faucet filter before you get involved with a more expensive installation. If you have mineral-laden hard water that makes it difficult to wash clothes and leaves ugly deposits on fixtures, install a water softener (see page 99).

WATER FILTRATION OPTIONS

Sediment — This option uses a filter to screen out particles that can clog your aerators and may make your water look cloudy. Usually, a sediment filter is used in conjunction with an activated-charcoal filter.

Activated-Charcoal — This filter will remove organic chemicals and pesticides. If your water is heavily chlorinated, it will remove much of the chlorine, improving the taste of your water. If taste is your major concern, install a small unit at the kitchen spout. A unit serving the whole house will need to have the charcoal filter replaced fairly frequently.

Reverse Osmosis — This is the most extreme measure, and it is capable of removing bacteria and harmful chemicals. It is expensive and bulky, requiring at least one holding tank. This system can be combined with an activated-charcoal system installed near the kitchen sink.

Water Softener — Also called an ion-exchange unit, this system will greatly reduce minerals such as calcium and iron. Have a water softener company install one for you—the piping is specialized and complicated.

INSTALLING WHOLE-HOUSE FILTERS

This typical whole-house system combines a sediment filter with an activated-charcoal unit. The plumbing is not complicated, but you will have to shut off water to the whole house before beginning. Also, you may have to reroute or raise pipes in order to gain enough room to install the two units.

YOU'LL NEED...
TIME: Half a day.
SKILLS: Good plumbing skills.
TOOLS: Wrenches and pliers, propane torch if you need to solder copper pipe.

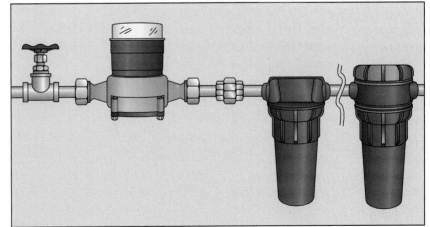

NOTE: *Shut off the water, and drain the line.* At a convenient point near the outlet side of the water meter (or just inside the house, if you have no meter), break into the line by opening a union or cutting the pipe (see pages 24, 84–85). Install a shutoff valve if you don't have one (see page 31). Remove 4 feet of pipe, and work toward the meter. If you wish, add a stop valve to cut off backflow when changing filters. Then install the charcoal filter, a nipple, and finally the sediment filter. Make the last joint with a union or sleeve coupling.

INSTALLING UNDER-SINK FILTRATION UNITS

A whole-house filtration system will supply you with filtered water in every tap and likely prolong the life of your water-using appliances. But because it is fairly difficult to install and requires regular filter changes, it is not installed by many homeowners. They reason that most of their water does not need to be treated, because it is used for bathing, flushing away waste, and washing clothes. They choose to filter the water that counts most, their drinking and cooking water.

You can install a unit that gives you filtered water every time you turn on the cold water at your kitchen sink, or you can install a separate faucet with the filter. The first type saves you the trouble of drilling a hole and installing a separate faucet. The separate faucet (installed much like the hot water dispenser on page 106) will mean that you will change filter cartridges less often.

Some systems include an activated-charcoal filter. This two-canister system takes a little more time to install but adds another stage of filtration.

Before you purchase a unit, measure your space under the sink, and make sure the new unit will fit. There are various types, but the connectors for all of them are fairly simple, ranging from standard compression fittings to simple connectors designed for a quick hookup to flexible supply lines. In most cases, you need only shut off the cold water supply, cut into a flexible supply, and install the system.

YOU'LL NEED...
TIME: Usually a half hour.
SKILLS: Basic plumbing skills.
TOOLS: Tubing cutter, flashlight, screwdriver.

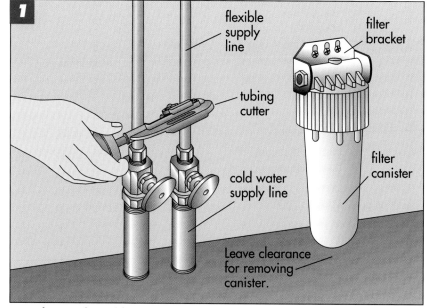

1. Filtering the cold water tap.
Anchor the filter in a location where you can get at it to replace its filter cartridges. Allow for enough clearance underneath to unscrew the canister when replacing cartridges. Use the screws provided to fasten it to the cabinet back or wall. If you do not have a flexible cold water supply line, install one (see pages 28 and 49). Cut into the cold water supply using a tubing cutter or plastic tubing cutter.

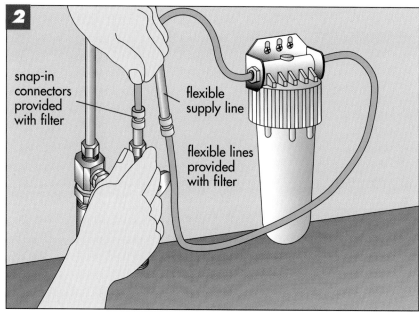

2. Hook up the filter.
Note which filter inlet is marked for the incoming supply, and connect that flexible tube to the section of supply line nearest the shutoff valve. For the connectors shown, you simply push the tubing in and they're joined. Connect the tube carrying filtered water to the section of flexible supply line for the faucet. Follow the manufacturer's directions for lubricating the canister seal and breaking in the system.

CHOOSING WATER SOFTENERS

A water softener removes minerals, especially iron, calcium, and magnesium, from water by means of ion exchange. As water passes through the unit, minerals are absorbed and replaced by sodium, which comes from salt that must be added to the storage tank from time to time.

The resulting soft water will clean clothes better than mineral-laden hard water, which does not create suds as readily. The drawback is that it adds salt to the water—probably not enough to damage your health, but enough to affect the taste of the water.

It is best to have a cold water bypass so some faucets receive unsoftened cold water. At the least, make sure your toilets and outside sill cocks do not receive softened water, or you will be paying for lots of extra salt.

In most cases, it pays to have a water softener service install and maintain your water softener. If you were to install one yourself, you would have to make drain and electrical connections, then periodically flush and recharge your system. With a service unit, the dealer simply brings a fresh tank and takes the old one to regenerate it.

In the unit shown, a bypass valve lets you or the dealer service the unit without shutting down your home's water supply.

EXPERTS' INSIGHT

FILTERING BACTERIA

If bacteria is your problem rather than simply minerals, sediment, taste, or odor, be careful which filter you choose. Some filters may actually increase the amount of bacteria in your drinking water because they remove chlorine. Bacteria can grow in dechlorinated water if it sits for a while, even if it's in your refrigerator.

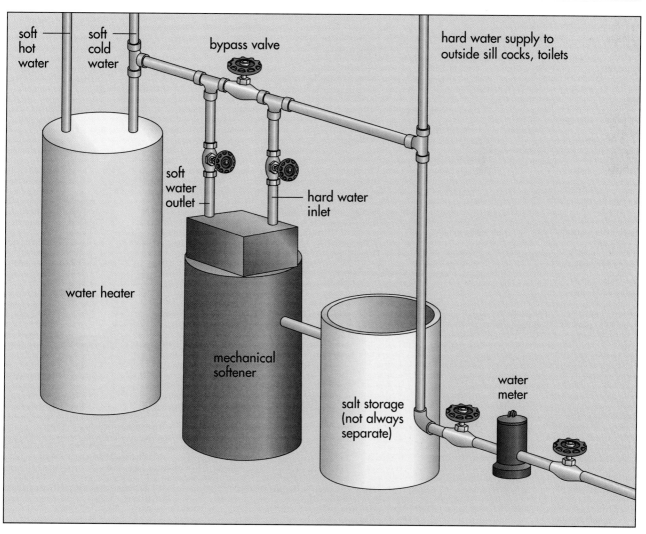

soft hot water

soft cold water

bypass valve

hard water supply to outside sill cocks, toilets

soft water outlet

hard water inlet

water heater

mechanical softener

salt storage (not always separate)

water meter

PLUMBING ICEMAKERS

If your refrigerator has an icemaker, supplying it with cold water is not difficult. The main problem will be to choose a path for the ¼-inch outside dimension flexible copper tubing. The cold water line under your kitchen sink may be the nearest source, but you may not be able to run the line so it isn't visible. If you have a basement, it's often easier to run the supply line through the floor to the pipes below.

YOU'LL NEED...

TIME: Several hours for an average installation.
SKILLS: Drilling holes, running flexible copper tubing without kinking it.
TOOLS: Drill, tongue-and-groove pliers or wrench, screwdriver.

EXPERTS' INSIGHT

ICEMAKER TIPS

■ Some localities may not allow saddle valves. If so, or if you are concerned that your water may clog up the tiny opening in a saddle valve, break into the line, and install a standard tee fitting, nipple, shutoff valve, and an adapter fitting.
■ If you don't like the taste of your water, purify the ice cubes the same way you purify your drinking water: Install a carbon filter prior to the icemaker line (see pages 97–98).
■ Even if you have flushed the line (Step 3), throw out the first two batches of ice to make sure the line is completely clean.

1. Install a saddle valve.
NOTE: *Shut off the water, and drain the line.* There are two types of saddle valves. One uses a spike to puncture the water supply pipe. You clamp it in place and twist the valve handle until it punctures the pipe. The other requires that you drill a hole in the line, twist the valve into the hole, and clamp the unit firmly on the pipe.

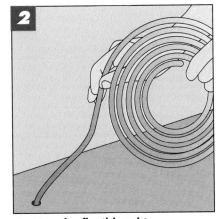

2. Run the flexible tubing.
Starting at the floor behind your refrigerator, drill a hole for the flexible copper line. Place it so the refrigerator will not bump into the line. Straighten the tubing carefully to avoid kinking it, and push it through the hole toward the saddle valve. Leave an ample amount of tubing in a springlike coil so you can pull the refrigerator out without kinking the tubing.

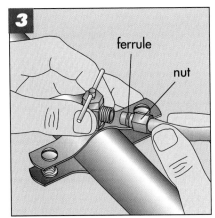

3. Connect to the saddle valve.
Taking care not to kink the tubing, bend it so you can stick it straight into the valve. Slip on a nut and ferrule, slide the tubing in, and tighten the nut. It is a good idea to flush the line before you start making ice. Place the other end of the tubing in a large bucket, and have a helper briefly turn the water back on to clear any sediment or burrs.

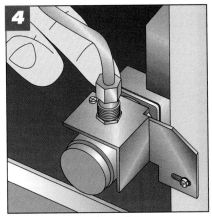

4. Connect to the refrigerator.
Position the refrigerator as if you were about to do that semiannual under-the-fridge floor cleaning. Carefully uncoil the tubing, and attach it to the icemaker connection as you did at the saddle valve. Turn on the valve at the refrigerator, and turn the water back on. If you used a drill-type saddle valve, open the saddle valve, and turn on the icemaker.

INSTALLING GARBAGE DISPOSALS

A garbage disposal is a useful upgrade to your kitchen that is not too difficult to install. The hardest part is working under your sink, so work on plenty of towels to make it as comfortable as possible. If you're installing a new sink, attach the disposal to the sink first, then set the sink in place. Begin by removing the trap from one of the sink strainers.

YOU'LL NEED...

TIME: Several hours, not including installing an electrical receptacle and switch.
SKILLS: Basic electrical and plumbing connections.
TOOLS: Hammer, spud wrench, screwdriver, tongue-and-groove pliers, putty knife, wire stripper.

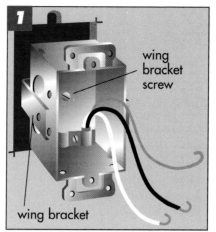

1. Supply electricity.
If there isn't one already, install an electrical box under the sink near the disposal. Install a GFCI receptacle, and plug the disposal in. Or, hard-wire the disposal (see Step 6 on page 102). Unless you are using a self-switching disposal, install a switch as well.

(see Step 6 on page 102)

TIME SAVER

SELF-SWITCHING DISPOSAL

■ Most disposals require a switched receptacle, leaving the homeowner with the difficult job of finding a good location for the switch. A wall switch usually means fishing an electrical line up the wall above the countertop. Another option is a switch on the face of the lower cabinets, but that puts it within the reach of children.

To avoid these problems, spend the extra money for a self-switching garbage disposal. Just plug it into a regular always hot receptacle. It turns on when food is pushed into it.

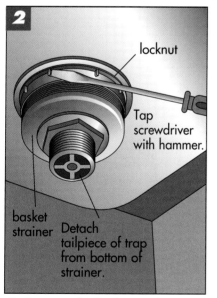

2. Remove the basket strainer.
Disconnect the trap assembly from the basket strainer and the drainpipe. Remove the locknut holding the strainer in place using a spud wrench or a hammer and screwdriver as shown. Lift out the strainer, and clean away old putty from around the sink opening using a putty knife, paint thinner, and an abrasive pad.

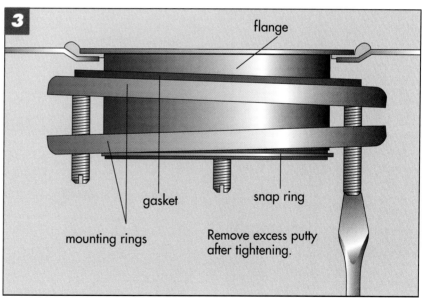

3. Install the mounting assembly.
You'll usually need to take apart the mounting assembly. To do this, remove the snap ring, mounting rings, and gasket from the flange.

Lay a rope of putty around the sink opening, and seat the flange in the opening. Have a helper hold the flange in place as you work from underneath. Slip the gasket, mounting rings, and snap ring up onto the flange. The snap ring will keep the mounting assembly in place temporarily.

Tighten the mounting assembly against the sink by turning the screws counterclockwise, as shown. Tighten each screw a little at a time to assure a tight seal. With a putty knife, shave away excess putty.

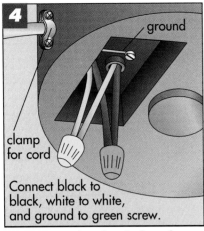

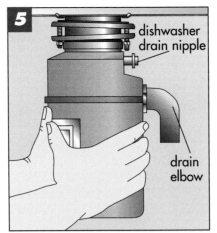

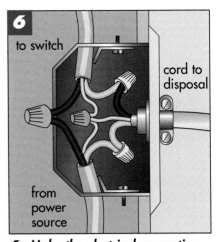

4. Connect the electrical cord.

Remove the electrical cover plate on the disposal. Strip sheathing and wire insulation from an approved appliance cord, and insert it into the opening. Tighten the clamp while holding the cord in place. Make the electrical connections in the disposal, gently push the wires into place, and reinstall the cover plate.

5. Attach the disposal.

Secure the drain elbow to the disposal. If you'll drain a dishwasher through the unit, remove the knockout inside the nipple. To mount the disposal, lift it into place, and rotate it until it engages and tightens. (This may take some muscle.) Once the connection is made, rotate the disposal to the best position for attaching the drain lines.

6. Make the electrical connection.
NOTE: *Shut off power.*
If you installed an electrical receptacle, simply insert the disposal's plug. For a hard-wired installation, connect the source black wire to the switch black wire, the white switch wire to the black wire leading to the disposal, the white disposal wire to the white power source wire, and all the ground wires together.

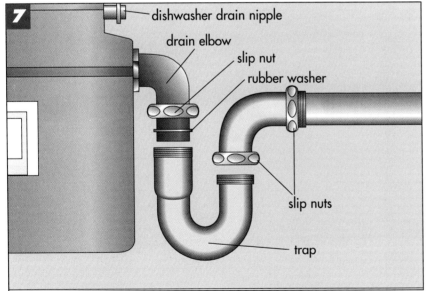

7. Connect the drain.

Fit a slip nut and a rubber washer onto the drain elbow, and fasten the trap to the elbow and the drainpipe. You may need to cut the elbow to make the connection. For double sinks, connect the elbow to the second bowl drain. If you will be draining a dishwasher through the disposal, connect the dishwasher drain hose to the drain nipple of the disposal. Use an automotive clamp to attach the hose, tightening it in place with a screwdriver or ratchet and socket. Test for leaks by running water down through the disposal. Turn the electrical power back on. With standing water in the bowl, turn the disposal on, and make sure it is securely attached.

EXPERTS' INSIGHT

TIPS ON INSTALLING THE DRAINPIPES

■ On a double-bowl sink, it is possible to remove the drain elbow of the disposal and run pipe straight across to the trap of the other bowl. But the best way is to install a separate trap for the disposal so each bowl has its own trap.

■ If the original drain traps are in good condition, reuse them. In most cases, if you buy one extension piece, you will have enough material to complete the piping. If your old trap looks at all worn, save yourself a repair job later by replacing it while you have everything apart.

MAINTAINING GARBAGE DISPOSALS

*T*o avoid maintenance problems, be sure you have cold water running before you turn on your disposal. Gradually feed in food waste, and do not stick a spatula or any silverware down past the splash guard. With the cold water continuing to flow, run the disposal for a few seconds after the food has been ground. If you hear a clanking sound, or if the disposal stops, remove the object that has caused the problem by following the steps shown here.

YOU'LL NEED...

TIME: Less than an hour to deal with most problems.
SKILLS: No special skills needed, unless you need to auger.
TOOLS: Allen wrench or disposal turning tool, flashlight, auger, broom handle.

Remove stuck objects.

If a fork, bottle cap, or any other solid object drops down through the splash guard, it can cause the disposal to jam. If this happens, turn off the power (if it has not already shut itself off). Remove the splash guard, and peer down the disposal with a flashlight. If you can't free the object, rotate the grinder with a broom handle.

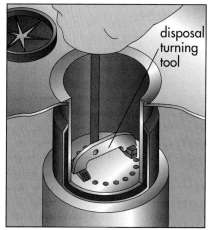

Use a special turning tool.

Your disposal may come with an Allen wrench that fits into a hole at the bottom of the disposal. If not, you can purchase a tool like the one shown. In either case, use the tool to turn the disposal back and forth. Once it's free, remove any obstructions, replace the splash guard, turn on the cold water, and test the disposal.

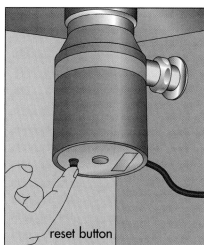

Reset an overloaded disposal.

If your disposal motor shuts off during operation, its overload protector has sensed overheating and has broken the electrical connection. Wait a few minutes for the unit to cool, then push the red reset button on the bottom of the disposal. If that doesn't work, check to see you have power to the unit by inspecting the cord and the fuse or circuit breaker.

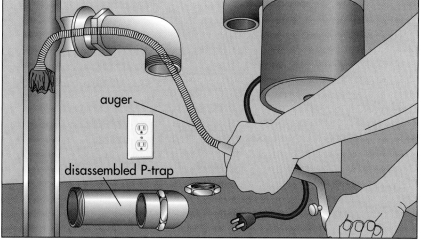

Disassemble and auger the drain.

Because a disposal gobbles up huge amounts of food waste, it's to be expected that occasionally the drain line will clog. If this happens, disassemble and remove the P-trap (make sure you have a bucket handy to catch the water that will spill), and clean out the trap (see page 72). If the trap itself is clear, thread a drain auger into the drainpipe (see page 74).

CAUTION

DON'T USE CHEMICALS

Do not attempt to clear a blocked drain line with chemicals of any type—not even "safe" chemicals. If the solution does not work, you'll be in danger of getting spattered with the stuff when you work to clear the line.

REPLACING AND INSTALLING DISHWASHERS

Replacing a dishwasher is fairly simple. Most units fit neatly into a 24-inch-wide undercounter cavity, and all are prewired and ready for simple supply, drainage, and electrical hookups. Installing a new dishwasher, however, is a much larger job: You must make room for it and bring in electrical, supply, and drain lines. To avoid straining the discharge pump, position the dishwasher as near to the sink as possible.

YOU'LL NEED...

TIME: About two hours to replace a dishwasher; a full day or more to put in a new one.
SKILLS: Simple electrical and plumbing skills for replacing; carpentry and basic plumbing and electrical skills for a new installation.
TOOLS: Drill, electrical tools, carpentry tools, screwdriver, tongue-and-groove pliers.

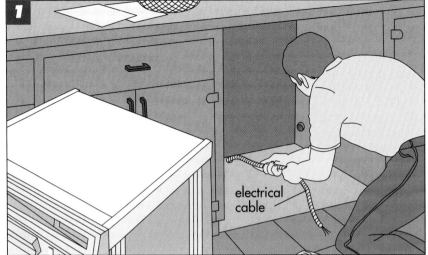

electrical cable

1. Prepare the opening.
NOTE: *Shut off the water, and shut off the electrical power.*
If you are replacing an existing dishwasher, remove its lower panel and disconnect the supply line, the drain hose, and the electrical line. Remove any screws attaching it to the countertop, and carefully pull the unit out.

For a new installation, remove a 24-inch-wide base cabinet, or tailor a space to fit the dishwasher. Bore a hole large enough to allow for the supply and drain lines near the lower back of the side panel of the adjoining cabinet. The dishwasher will need its own 15- or 20-amp circuit. Run a circuit from the service panel (you may want to hire a licensed electrician to install this).

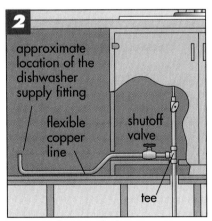

approximate location of the dishwasher supply fitting

flexible copper line

shutoff valve

tee

2. Run the supply line.
Cut into the hot water supply line, and insert a standard tee fitting, a nipple, and a shutoff valve. Run flexible copper tubing into the cavity, leaving enough line to reach the dishwasher supply fitting. (See pages 24–27 and 84–85 for information on working with various types of pipes.)

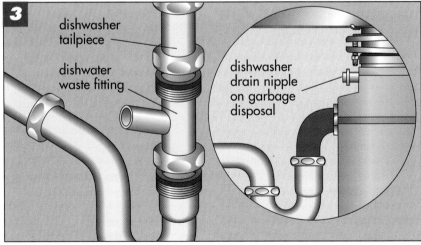

dishwasher tailpiece

dishwater waste fitting

dishwasher drain nipple on garbage disposal

3. Provide a drain fitting.
Your dishwasher can drain either into the sink drain or into a garbage disposal if you have one.

For sink drainage, install a dishwasher tailpiece. Loosen the slip nuts and remove the tailpiece, insert the dishwasher tailpiece into the trap, and cut the old tailpiece to fit above it. Connect all the pieces, and tighten the slip nuts.

To drain a dishwasher into a garbage disposal, use a screwdriver and hammer to remove the metal knockout inside the dishwasher drain nipple located near the top of the disposal. The knockout, when freed, may fall into the grinding chamber of the disposal, so be sure to take it out.

4. Attach the drain line.

Thread the drain line through the hole in the cabinet, and slip it onto the dishwasher tailpiece or drain nipple—you may have to push hard. Secure it with an automotive hose clamp.

To ensure proper operation of the appliance, the drain line must make a loop as shown at top right, so that at some point it is raised near the height of the countertop. Support the drain line securely—it will vibrate during use—by wrapping a couple of lengths of wire around it and fastening them to screws driven into the underside of the countertop. Take care that the screws do not poke through the countertop.

Some local codes require an air gap (see inset) at the top of the loop. You can place this in a knockout hole in the sink, or drill a hole for it in the countertop. Run one line from the drain nipple to the air gap, another from the air gap to the dishwasher drain outlet.

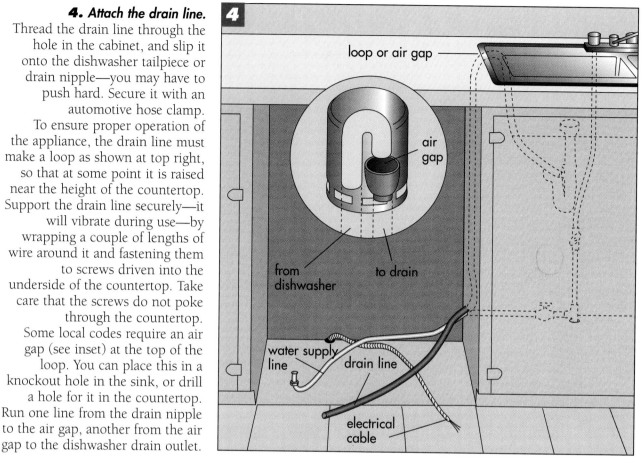

5. Make the hookups.

Position the ends of the three lines approximately at the locations where they will be connected to the dishwasher. Remove the bottom cover plate from the dishwasher, and slide the unit carefully into place, watching to make sure no lines are damaged. Make sure the dishwasher is all the way in position.

Make the connections as shown in the detail drawings. Tighten the compression nut and drain line clamp firmly, and make secure electrical connections.

Level the dishwasher by turning the leveling screws on the legs. Anchor the dishwasher to the underside of the countertop with screws. Turn on the water and the electrical power. Before reattaching access panels, run the washer, watching carefully for leaks.

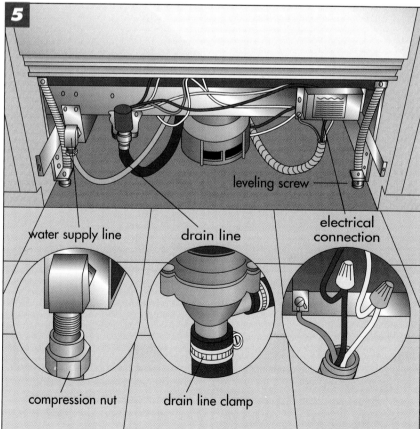

INSTALLING HOT WATER DISPENSERS

With this appliance, you can have an immediate source of piping hot water for instant soup, tea, and coffee, as well as for quick blanching of vegetables.

Installation is relatively simple. The most difficult step will likely be adding an electrical receptacle under the sink. You can't use the receptacle for your garbage disposal, because it's switched; this one must be live all the time.

When you open the faucet valve, unheated water enters the dispenser through the supply tube, warming as it passes through the expansion chamber. The pressure of the incoming water forces hot water from the holding tank and expansion chamber (where it cools to 200°) out the spout. When the temperature in the tank drops, a thermostat activates heating elements to return the water to the correct temperature.

YOU'LL NEED...

TIME: About three hours, not including installation of an electrical receptacle.
SKILLS: Drilling a clean hole, careful handling of flexible line, electrical skills.
TOOLS: Drill, holesaw or metal-boring holesaw, screwdriver, tongue-and-groove pliers, wire strippers.

1. Wire a receptacle.

If you do not have one already, install a grounded electrical receptacle that is always live under the sink, near the location of the dispenser. If your unit has a plug, codes require that a GFCI receptacle be used anywhere within 6 feet of a water source. (See page 101 for installing the receptacle box.)

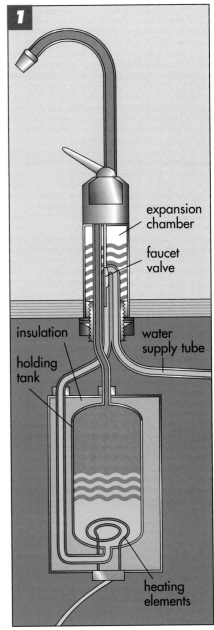

expansion chamber

faucet valve

insulation

water supply tube

holding tank

heating elements

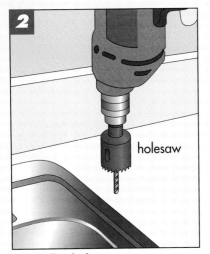

holesaw

2. Drill a hole.

Decide where you want to place the dispenser. It is often easiest to drill a hole near the back edge of the countertop near the sink, using a fine-toothed holesaw. Make sure you leave room for the entire diameter of the unit. Position the hole so the faucet is close enough to the sink.

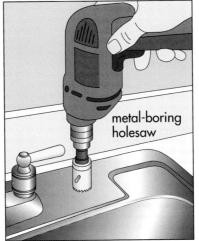

metal-boring holesaw

Your sink may have a knockout hole. If it's the right size, just punch the insert out from below.

If you have a stainless-steel sink, you can buy a holesaw designed to cut through metal. Drill slowly. If you are installing a new sink, select one with an extra hole.

CAUTION!
CHECK YOUR CIRCUIT

Any heating element draws a lot of current. If your circuit is already overloaded, you may need to have an electrician install a grounded circuit for this unit. If your unit has a plug, be sure to install a ground-fault circuit-interrupter (GFCI) receptacle as well.

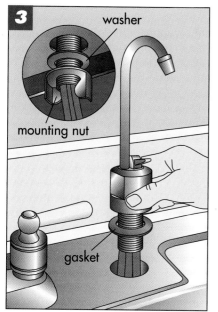

3. Attach the faucet assembly.
Insert the assembly with its gasket into the hole. You may need a helper to hold the dispenser in the correct position as you crawl underneath and work. Slip on the washer, screw on the mounting nut, and tighten firmly.

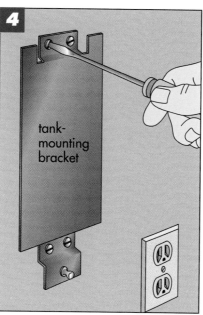

4. Mount the tank.
Use screws to fasten the tank mounting bracket to the wall. Make sure the bracket is plumb. Place it 12 to 14 inches below the underside of the countertop. Mount the tank onto the bracket.

EXPERTS' INSIGHT

MAINTAINING YOUR HOT WATER DISPENSER

■ After a dispenser is installed, water may drip from the spout even when the valve is off. If this happens, lower the thermostat setting—pressure from water that is too hot can force water past the valve.

■ If you plan to not use the dispenser for a period of time, unplug it or switch it off, close off the water supply valve, and drain the unit of water.

■ Take care when you use your dispenser—the water is indeed hot. Instruct children not to use it. Be sure to keep flammable items—such as shopping bags and rags—well away from the holding tank under the sink.

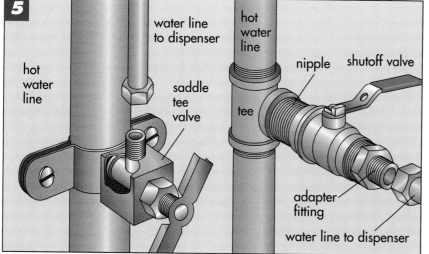

5. Install a water-supply valve.
NOTE: *Shut off the water, and drain the line.* To supply the unit with water, tap into the hot water line serving the sink. If codes permit, the easy way is with a saddle tee valve. Don't use the puncture-type saddle tee. Although it is easier to install, it clogs easily. Instead, drill a small hole in the supply line, then secure the clamp to the line

as shown here. If saddle tees are not allowed in your locality, you'll have some plumbing to do. Break into the line (see page 25), and install a standard tee fitting. Add a nipple and a shutoff valve as shown on the right. You'll need an adapter fitting to make the transition to a flexible water line that matches your dispenser's supply line.

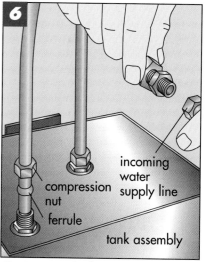

6. Connect the lines.
Secure the two longer tubes to the tank assembly and the shorter one to the water supply tube by tightening a compression nut and ferrule onto each threaded fitting. The longer tubes will be coded to make it clear where each goes. Restore water pressure, and check for leaks. Let the tank fill before plugging in or turning on the unit.

GLOSSARY

For words not listed here, or for more about those that are, refer to the index (pages 110–112).

Access panel. A removable panel in a wall or ceiling that permits repair or replacement of concealed items such as faucet bodies.

Adapter. A fitting that makes it possible to go from male endings to female endings or vice-versa. Transition adapters allow for joining different kinds of pipe together in the same run. Trap adapters help connect drain lines to sink traps.

Aerator. A device screwed into the spout outlet of most sink faucets that mixes air with the water to achieve less water splash and smoother flow.

Air chamber. A short, enclosed tube on water lines that provides a cushion of air to control sudden surges in water pressure that sometimes result in noisy pipes.

Auger. A flexible metal cable fished into traps and drain lines to dislodge obstructions.

Ballcock. The assembly inside a toilet tank that, when activated, releases water into the bowl to start the flushing action. It also prepares the toilet for the subsequent flushes.

Capillary action. The action that occurs when a liquid is drawn into a razor-thin space between two almost-touching solid surfaces, such as when molten solder is drawn into and around a copper pipe joint.

Clean-out. A removable plug in a trap or a drainpipe that allows easier access to blockages inside.

Closet bend. The elbow-shaped fitting beneath toilets that carries waste to the main drain.

Codes. *See* Uniform Plumbing Code.

Coupling. A fitting used to connect two lengths of pipe in a straight run.

Drain-waste-vent (DWV) system. The network of pipes and fittings that carries liquid and solid wastes out of a building to a public sewer, a septic tank, or a cesspool. It also allows for the passage of sewer gases up through the roof and to the outside.

Elbow. A fitting used to change the direction of a water supply line. Also known as an ell. Bends do the same thing with drain-waste-vent lines.

Fall. Used to express the slope at which drain lines are installed to ensure proper waste drainage. Minimum fall per foot is $\frac{1}{4}$ inch.

Fitting. Any connector (except a valve) that allows you to join pipes of similar or dissimilar size or material in a straight run or at an angle.

Fixture. Any of several devices that provide a supply of water or sanitary disposal of liquid or solid wastes. Tubs, showers, sinks, and toilets are examples.

Fixture drain. The drainpipe and trap leading from a fixture to the main drain.

Flux. A stiff jelly brushed or smeared on the surfaces of copper and brass pipes and fittings before soldering them to assist in the cleaning and bonding processes.

Force cup. *See* Plunger.

Increaser. A fitting used to enlarge a vent stack as it passes through the roof.

Inside diameter (ID). Almost all plumbing pipes are sized according to their inside diameter. *See also* Nominal size *and* Outside Diameter.

Main drain. That portion of the drainage system between the fixture drains and the sewer drain. *See also* Fixture drain *and* Sewer drain.

Nipple. A 12-inch or shorter pipe that has threads on both ends that is used to join fittings. A close nipple has threads that run from both ends to the center.

No-hub pipe. A type of cast-iron pipe designed for use by do-it-yourselfers. Pipes and fittings are joined using stainless-steel clamps with rubber gaskets.

Nominal size. The designated dimension of a pipe or fitting. It varies slightly from the actual size. *See also* Inside diameter.

O-ring. A round rubber washer used to create a watertight seal, chiefly around valve stems.

Outside diameter (OD). Plumbing parts are rarely measured by their outside diameter, with flexible copper tubing being the primary exception. *See also* Inside diameter *and* Nominal size.

Packing. An asbestos material (used mainly around faucet stems) that, when compressed, results in a watertight seal.

Pipe joint compound. A material applied to pipe threads to ensure a watertight seal. Also called pipe dope. *See also* Teflon tape.

Plumber's putty. A doughlike material used as a sealant. Often a bead of it is around the underside of toilets and sinks.

Plunger. A suction-action tool used to dislodge obstructions from drain lines. Also called a force cup and a plumber's friend.

PSI. The abbreviation for pounds per square inch. Water pressure is rated in PSIs.

Reducer. A fitting with different-size openings at either end used to go from a larger to a smaller pipe.

Relief valve. A device designed to open if it senses excess temperature or pressure.

Rough-in. The early stages of a plumbing project during which supply and drain-waste-vent lines are run to their destinations. All work done after the rough-in is finish work.

Run. Any length of pipe or pipes and fittings going in a straight line.

Saddle tee. A fitting used to tap into a water line without having to break the line apart. Some local codes prohibit its use.

Sanitary fitting. Any of several connectors used to join drain-waste-vent lines. Their design helps direct waste downward.

Sanitary sewer. Underground drainage network that carries liquid and solid waste to a treatment plant.

Septic tank. A reservoir that collects and separates liquid and solid wastes, diverting the liquid waste onto a drainage field.

Sewer drain. That part of the drainage system that carries liquid and solid waste from a dwelling to a sanitary sewer, septic tank, or cesspool.

Soil stack. A vertical drainpipe that carries waste toward the sewer drain. The main soil stack is the largest vertical drain line of a building into which liquid and solid waste from branch drains flow. *See also* Vent stack.

Soldering. A technique used to produce watertight joints between various types of metal pipes and fittings. Solder, when reduced to molten form by heat, fills the void between two metal surfaces and joins them together.

Solvent-welding. A technique used to produce watertight joints between plastic pipes and fittings. Chemical "cement" softens mating surfaces temporarily and enables them to meld into one.

Stop valve. A device installed in a water supply line, usually near a fixture, that lets you shut off the water supply to one fixture without interrupting service to the rest of the system.

Storm sewer. An underground drainage network designed to collect and carry away water coming into it from storm drains. *See also* Sanitary sewer.

Tailpiece. That part of a fixture drain that bridges the gap between the drain outlet and the trap.

Tee. A T-shaped fitting used to tap into a length of pipe at a 90-degree angle for the purposes of beginning a branch line.

Teflon tape. A synthetic material wrapped around pipe threads to seal a joint. Often called pipe tape. *See also* Pipe joint compound.

Trap. The part of a fixture drain that creates a water seal to prevent sewer gases from penetrating a home's interior. Codes require that all fixtures be trapped.

Uniform Plumbing Code. A nationally recognized set of guidelines prescribing safe plumbing practices. Local codes take precedence over this when the two differ.

Union. A fitting used in runs of threaded pipe to facilitate disconnecting the line without having to cut it.

Vent. The vertical or sloping horizontal portion of a drain line that permits sewer gases to exit the house. Every fixture in a house must be vented.

Vent stack. The upper portion of a vertical drain line through which gases pass directly to the outside. The main vent stack is the portion of the main vertical drain line above the highest fixture connected to it.

Water hammer. A loud noise caused by a sudden stop in the flow of water, which causes pipes to repeatedly hit up against a nearby framing member.

Water supply system. The network of pipes and fittings that transports water under pressure to fixtures and other water-using equipment and appliances.

Wet wall. A strategically placed cavity (usually a 2×6 wall) in which the main drain/vent stack and a cluster of supply and drain-waste-vent lines are housed.

Wye. A Y-shaped drainage fitting that serves as the starting point for a branch drain supplying one or more fixtures.

INDEX

A–B

Adapters, 14, 15, 89
Aerators, 48
Air chambers, 29
Augering, 70, 71, 74–77
Ball valves, 31
Bathtubs. *See* Tubs
Bend fittings, 14, 15
Black steel pipe. *See*
    Threaded pipe
Buffalo box, 6

C

Cartridge faucets, 40–41, 67
Cast-iron pipe
    cutting, 87
    dimensions, 16
    leak repairs, 35
    tapping into, 87
    uses and features, 12–13
Clamps, pipe, 34
Clean-outs, 8, 35, 77
Closet augers, 76
Closet flanges, 14, 15, 56, 57
Codes, building, 4, 80, 81, 88
Compression fittings, 22, 30
Copper pipe
    advantages of, 6, 7
    cutting, 18
    dimensions, 16
    flexible, 21, 23, 49, 51, 100
    measuring, 17
    soldering rigid, 18–20
    uses and features, 12–13
Couplings, 14, 15

D–E

Disk faucets, 44–45
Dishwashers, 71, 104–105
Diverter valves, 48, 66
Drain lines. *See also* Venting
    assemblies, 51, 68, 71, 78, 90
    clogged, 70–72, 74–77

dishwasher, 105
drain-waste-vent (DWV)
    systems, 6, 8, 9
  garbage disposal, 102, 103
  hidden pipes, locating, 82
  main drains, 77
  pipe choices, 12–13
  planning new, 80–83
  plastic pipe, 86
  sewer, 77
  tapping into, 84–87
  toilet, 56
  tub, 68, 69
Electrical connections
  dishwasher, 105
  garbage disposal, 101, 102
  hot water dispenser, 106
  water heater, 60, 65
Ells (elbows), 14, 15, 89

F

Faucets
  aerators, 48
  base plates, 47
  cartridge, 40–41, 67
  disk, 44–45
  diverter valves, 48, 66
  gasketed cartridge, 46
  leak repairs, 37–47, 67
  replacing, 50–51
  rotating ball, 42–43, 67
  seats, 36, 37, 39
  sprayers, 48, 51
  stem, 36–39, 66
  tub and shower, 66–67
  washers, 36, 37, 39
  water supply lines, 49, 50, 51
Ferrules, 22, 49
Fittings
  compression, 22, 28
  copper pipe, 18, 19, 20
  flare, 23
  measuring, 17
  plastic pipe, 26–27, 28
  sanitary, 14, 15, 81, 84, 86
  threaded pipe, 25
  types of, 14–15

Flare fittings, 23
Flexible tubing
  copper, 21, 23, 49, 51, 100
  plastic, 28, 49
Flux, 19
Frozen pipes, 32–35

G–K

Galvanized pipe
  disadvantages of, 6, 7
  installing, 25
  removing, 24
  uses and features, 12–13
Garbage disposals, 101–103
Gasketed cartridge faucets, 46
Gas lines, 12
Gate valves, 31
Globe valves, 31
Heat tape, electrical, 32
Hot water dispensers, 106–107
Icemakers, 100
Inspectors, building, 4
Insulating pipes, 29, 32

L–Q

Leaks
  faucet, 37–47
  flexible supply line, 49
  main shutoff valve, 31
  pipe, 34–35
  sink, 73
  toilet, 53–55
  tub and shower controls, 67
  water heater, 59
Nipples, 14, 15, 25
No-hub fittings, 15, 87
Noisy pipes, 29
Pipe. *See also* Cast-iron pipe;
    Copper pipe; Plastic pipe;
    Threaded pipe
  clamps, 34
  cutting, 18, 26, 86, 87
  for drain lines, 8
  hangers, 20
  insulating, 29, 32
  measuring, 16–17

replacing old, 6, 24
sizes, 12, 16
soldering, 18–20
types of, 12–13
for water heater lines, 63
Plastic pipe
advantages of, 6, 7
cutting, 26, 86
dimensions, 16
drain lines, 86
flexible, 28, 49
measuring, 17
rigid, 26–27
uses and features, 12–13
Plunging, 10, 71, 76
Pop-up drain assemblies,
51, 71, 78

R–S
Rotating ball faucets, 42–43, 67
Sanitary fittings, 14, 15,
81, 84, 86
Sewer line clogs, 77
Showers
clogged drains, 74
controls, 66–67, 83
hand shower installation, 96
installing, 94–95
prefab stalls, 94, 95
roughing in new, 82–83
showerheads, 79
tile installation, 95
Shutoff valves, 6, 7, 31
Sill cocks, 7, 32
Sinks
anatomy of, 70
clogged drains, 70–72
drain assemblies, 51, 71, 78
installing
pedestal, 93
rimmed, 90–91
vanity, 93
wall-hung, 92
removing, 90, 92
roughing in new, 82–83
strainers, 73, 91

Soil pipe, 8
Soldering copper pipe, 18–20
Sprayers, 48, 51
Stacks. *See* Venting
Steel pipe. *See* Threaded pipe
Stem faucets
sink, 36, 37–39
tub and shower, 66
Stop valves, 7, 30
Supply lines. *See* Water
supply lines

T
Tees, 14, 15, 84, 85, 86
Threaded pipe
dimensions, 16
galvanized, 6, 7, 12–13
installing, 25
measuring, 17
removing, 24
uses and features, 12–13
Tile installation, 95
Toilets
anatomy of, 52
clogged, 76
closet flanges, 14, 15, 56, 57
drains, 56
flush tank repairs, 53–54
leak repairs, 53–55
overflows, 76
Repair Chart, 53
replacing, 56–57
roughing in new, 82–83
seat installation, 57
water-saving, 57
water supply lines, 55, 57
winterizing, 33
Tools
augers, 70, 71
essential, 10

flaring, 11, 23
pipe cutters, 87
seat grinders and wrenches, 39
specialized, 11
tubing cutters, 11,18, 21, 28
Transition fittings, 14, 15
Traps
adapters for, 14, 15
dismantling, 72
drum, 75
garbage disposal, 103
house, 77
purpose of, 8
toilet, 76
Trip-lever drain assemblies, 78
Tubing. *See* Flexible tubing
Tubs
clogged, 75
controls, 66–67
drain assemblies, 68, 78
replacing, 68–69
roughing in new, 82–83

U–V
Uniform Plumbing Code, 4
Union fittings, 14, 15, 24, 25
Valves
brass, 20
diverter, 48, 66
main shutoff, 6, 7, 31
saddle, 100
stop, 7, 30
water heater, 59, 63
Venting
adding new, 88
flashing, 88
reventing, 80, 81, 88
systems, 6, 9
tapping into, 80–81, 84–87
waste stacks, 8

W–Z
Wall finishing, 69, 92, 95
Washers, 36, 37, 39
Water filters, 97–98, 99

flaring, 11, 23
pipe cutters, 87
seat grinders and wrenches, 39
specialized, 11
tubing cutters, 11,18, 21, 28
Transition fittings, 14, 15
Traps
adapters for, 14, 15
dismantling, 72
drum, 75
garbage disposal, 103
house, 77

purpose of, 8
toilet, 76
Trip-lever drain assemblies, 78
Tubing. *See* Flexible tubing
Tubs
clogged, 75
controls, 66–67
drain assemblies, 68, 78
replacing, 68–69
roughing in new, 82–83

Uniform Plumbing Code, 4
Union fittings, 14, 15, 24, 25
Valves
brass, 20
diverter, 48, 66
main shutoff, 6, 7, 31
saddle, 100
stop, 7, 30
water heater, 59, 63
Venting
adding new, 88
flashing, 88

U–V

METRIC CONVERSIONS

U.S. UNITS TO METRIC EQUIVALENTS			METRIC UNITS TO U.S. EQUIVALENTS		
To Convert From	Multiply By	To Get	To Convert From	Multiply By	To Get
Inches	25.4	Millimetres	Millimetres	0.0394	Inches
Inches	2.54	Centimetres	Centimetres	0.3937	Inches
Feet	30.48	Centimetres	Centimetres	0.0328	Feet
Feet	0.3048	Metres	Metres	3.2808	Feet
Yards	0.9144	Metres	Metres	1.0936	Yards
Miles	1.6093	Kilometres	Kilometres	0.6214	Miles
Square inches	6.4516	Square centimetres	Square centimetres	0.1550	Square inches
Square feet	0.0929	Square metres	Square metres	10.764	Square feet
Square yards	0.8361	Square metres	Square metres	1.1960	Square yards
Acres	0.4047	Hectares	Hectares	2.4711	Acres
Square miles	2.5899	Square kilometres	Square kilometres	0.3861	Square miles
Cubic inches	16.387	Cubic centimetres	Cubic centimetres	0.0610	Cubic inches
Cubic feet	0.0283	Cubic metres	Cubic metres	35.315	Cubic feet
Cubic feet	28.316	Litres	Litres	0.0353	Cubic feet
Cubic yards	0.7646	Cubic metres	Cubic metres	1.308U	Cubic yards
Cubic yards	764.55	Litres	Litres	0.0013	Cubic yards
Fluid ounces	29.574	Millilitres	Millilitres	0.0338	Fluid ounces
Quarts	0.9464	Litres	Litres	1.0567	Quarts
Gallons	3.7854	Litres	Litres	0.2642	Gallons
Drams	1.7718	Grams	Grams	0.5644	Drams
Ounces	28.350	Grams	Grams	0.0353	Ounces
Pounds	0.4536	Kilograms	Kilograms	2.2046	Pounds
To convert from degrees Fahrenheit (F) to degrees Celsius (C), first subtract 32, then multiply by ⁵⁄₉.			To convert from degrees Celsius to degrees Fahrenheit, multiply by ⁹⁄₅, then add 32.		